Dickens and Reality

DICKENS
And
Reality

John Romano

Columbia University Press   New York

1978

The Andrew W. Mellon Foundation, through a special grant, has assisted the Press in publishing this volume.

Library of Congress Cataloging in Publication Data
Romano, John, 1948–
Dickens and reality.
Bibliography: p.
Includes index.
1. Dickens, Charles, 1812–1870—Criticism and interpretation.
2. Realism in literature.   I. Title.
PR4588.R6   823'.8   77-10745
ISBN 0-231-04246-9

Columbia University Press
New York   Guildford, Surrey
Copyright © 1975, 1978 Columbia University Press / All rights reserved
Printed in the United States of America

For my Mother

... and for Nancy

Contents

Acknowledgments

I wish to thank Professor J. Hillis Miller of Yale University, most critical and most open-minded of thesis advisers, who guided me in the preparation of the original version of this study. Thanks are also due to my other teachers in New Haven: to Charles Feidelson, Jr., Charles Long, and Martin Price, and especially to David Thorburn; also to Frederick Busch and Jonathan Kistler of Colgate University; to my argumentative friends John Crigler and Robert Yeager; and to Raymond Hartung. Among my colleagues at Columbia, Steven Marcus and Michael Wood have read parts of the manuscript and offered useful suggestions for which I am grateful.

I wish to thank the Danforth Foundation and the Columbia Council for the Humanities for their generosity.

While I was revising this work for publication, my beloved wife, Nancy Forbes, offered continual assistance and support.

Note on Editions of Dickens' Works

Except for novels which as of this writing appeared as volumes of the Clarendon Dickens, I have preferred the paperback Penguin editions to the Oxford Illustrated Dickens, which has sometimes been regarded as standard. The Penguin, at least, informs the reader of the date and relative authority of the text it uses, and sometimes includes significant variants as well. Thus references to the novels studied in the following pages are to these editions:

Oliver Twist, ed. Kathleen Tillotson, Clarendon Ed. (Oxford: Clarendon, 1966).

The Old Curiosity Shop, ed. Angus Easson (Harmondsworth: Penguin Books, 1972). Introduction by Malcolm Andrews.

Dombey and Son, ed. Alan Horsman, Clarendon Ed. (Oxford: Clarendon, 1974).

Little Dorrit, ed. John Holloway (Harmondsworth: Penguin Books, 1967).

Our Mutual Friend, ed. Stephen Gill (Harmondsworth: Penguin Books, 1971).

References are to book, chapter, page: (i, i, 1).

Dickens and Reality

"Upon your word no isn't there I never did but that's like me I run away with an idea and having none to spare I keep it, alas there was a time dear Arthur that is to say decidedly not dear nor Arthur neither but you understand me when one bright idea gilded the what's-his-name horizon of et cetera but it is darkly clouded now and all is over."

—*Little Dorrit*

Introduction

The Horizon of Etcetera

From Lausanne, in 1846, Charles Dickens wrote home to his biographer, John Forster, about a friendship he had struck up with a young patient at the public asylum for the blind: "He is very fond of smoking. I have arranged to supply him with cigars during our stay here; so he and I are in amazing sympathy. I don't know whether he thinks I grow them, or make them, or produce them by winking, or what. But it gives him a notion that the world in general belongs to me." [1]

As Dickens' readers, we are recipients of another kind of gift from his magical bounty, and we share in the blind man's amazement. We know how hard it is to know where Dickens got what he gave us. Certainly he seems to have produced the vast panorama of his fiction from his observation of a world to which the rest of us are blind. Was it a world that belonged exclusively to Dickens, as the young Swiss is fancifully said to have supposed, or was it the world Dickens shared with his contemporaries and with ourselves, although he took it in through keener senses? This is no easy question to answer in our blindness.

But if one answer has been favored over another in recent years, it has been that Dickens winked his creations into being. Another way of saying this is that "we" do not think of Dickens as a realist. The question of what world Dickens drew upon has become moot in our consensus that the world he created and ceded to us in such bulk is an unreal and imaginary one, "belonging" to Dickens: There are real things in it, but they have been transmogrified in having gone the distance from the real world to Dickens' own.

Not a little historical irony attaches to this consensus. The progress of Dickens' career as a novelist and the rise of realism in the fiction of the last century were almost exactly contemporary phenomena, and both were triumphant. When the historical issue of realism rather than its aesthetic is under discussion, one frequently if not usually finds Dickens named among the great artists of that persuasion, as he is by critics as diverse as George Lukács and René Wellek.[2] His influence on writers normally regarded as realists, such as Turgenieff, Tolstoy, and even Henry James, has been acknowledged for a long time.[3] But the high critical estimate of Dickens' novels today is largely based on an appreciation of those aspects which are least realistic in the ordinary sense: their grotesquerie and "expressionism," their self-conscious symbolism and "myth-making," or their spiritual and artistic affinities with the "higher realism" of Dostoyevsky or the frank irreality of Kafka. When we read Dickens beside the work of an orthodox realist like Tolstoy, despite what we may know of Dickens' influence on the latter, we are struck by the distance of the "world" of Dickens' novels from our own world, the "real" world in which Tolstoy's fiction overtly pretends to take place.[4] While Tolstoy endeavors to reconcile his details of plot and character, time and place, to historical fact or to familiar human experience, the details of a Dickens novel, by and large, seem reconciled primarily to each other, cohering at last in a significant whole but responsible along the way to no expectations derived from experience outside the text.

Such a reading of Dickens—and I am assuming it is the standard one—has been useful in freeing the appreciation of his art from standards irrelevant to its aims and methods, such as those inherent in the approach to fiction of James and Jamesians. At the same time, a single-minded stress on the separation of Dickens' fictive world from our own slights the realistic or representational elements in the novels and their persistent claim, like the claim in Tolstoy, that they are set in the real world. This claim is advanced in some obvious ways, which will be recognized as constituting those aspects of the novels that what I am calling the standard interpretation is inclined to ignore, for example, their intense topicality, their reformist or simply descriptive journalism, their frequently dense specificity of detail in familiar and "typical" settings. Also perhaps the claim of realism is corollary to the emotional claims the novels make upon us, now held suspect under the rubric of "sentimentalism." We care about the fate of characters because we accept, in some way, the idea that they are real.

But a novel can of course be wrong about itself, and it is open to a critic to say that a novel fails to be realistic, however many "claims" to realism it puts forward. He will be especially inclined to say so about a novel by Dickens if his notion of realism in literature descends from Ian Watt's influential formulation of twenty years ago.[5] To Watt, realism means "realism of presentation": "The novel's realism resides not in the kind of life it presents, but in the way it presents it," not in its themes nor in the cumulative conveyance of meaning by action, character, and setting, language and "form," but in the lifelikeness and verisimilitude of its details.[6] It is interesting that Watt actually uses the term "formal realism" more often than "presentational." By it, he means the realism characteristic of the novel as a genre, constituting in his view the central tradition of its historical development. Thus equating "form" with genre, he disregards the technical definition of form developed by the New Critics in the decade previous to his writing, as naming the constitutive literary object itself, the complex and signifying whole of a specific work. The relations between realism and the novel "form" in this latter sense receive no explicit attention in Watt's essay. And yet in order to comprehend Dickens' status as a realist, it may be necessary to remove the emphasis from presentation, and place it on questions of form. The formalist revision in criticism ignored in Watt's essay was, after all, very important for Dickens criticism. With its description of the work of art as "a world in itself of illusion and symbolic forms," it provided a setting for the sympathetic portrayal of Dickens the symbolist that appeared in the widely known work of Lionel Trilling and Dorothy Van Ghent in the 1950's.[7] As will appear shortly, I am far from believing that formalism itself can give an adequate account of the work of Dickens, or of any novelist whose affinities with realism are significant. But our understanding of Dickens has consistently benefited from the discussion, at least, of how literary works "cohere" and "correspond," or fail to; and there is no reason why my present purpose should prove exceptional.

Therefore I begin by examining, in chapter 1, what I take to be a crux or paradigm of form at the beginning of what is perhaps the greatest realist novel. From it I derive some general questions about the relation of realism to the novel form, and especially, by means of a comparison with similar material in *Our Mutual Friend,* about realism and the form of Dickens' novels. The next chapter continues the discussion of *Our Mutual Friend* to show that the notion of realist form has recognizable and important implications for other than formal matters—in particular, for the themes of the novel, as well as for its characters and its means of characterization. In chapter 3, the developing idea is brought to bear upon a consideration of language in the Dickens novel. For that purpose, passages from *Little Dorrit, Dombey and Son,* and *The Old Curiosity Shop* are closely examined. *Oliver Twist,* in the chapter that follows, provides an opportunity not only to extend the argument to an earlier Dickens but also to take up two questions of obvious relevance to the issue of Dickens' realism: the charge of sentimentality, and the aesthetic of the novel of social protest. In the conclusion, *Dombey and Son* is called Dickens' "novel of reality," but by then it will be clear, I hope, that the novel of reality is indeed the novel Dickens is always writing.

Beyond that reading of Dickens with which I am primarily concerned, it is my hope to contribute something toward the understanding of realism itself, as a historical movement and as a topic in literary aesthetics that is always at issue. Discussions of this subject sometimes founder because it is assumed that we cannot discuss what we cannot define—a sensible-sounding assumption that is not always just. "Realism," as it happens, is one of many important and useful terms that defy methodical definition, and become, in fact, less useful as the diversity of their possible meanings is restricted. It would be historically disingenuous to attempt to detach the word from the long and contradictory history of its use, from neo-Platonist philosophy through the ideological wars of art criticism in the last century. Moreover, that matrix of contradictions is itself richer and more suggestive than any distillation could be. For example, it might seem possible for the literary critic to ignore the medieval neo-Platonists who meant by realism a belief in the actual existence of ideal abstractions; but mention of that usage is helpful in cautioning us against too easy an equation of realism with the presentation of concrete, material details, an equation to which we are dangerously prone.[8] We say of a portrait by Franz Hals, or Courbet, or Andrew Wyeth that it is realistic because it renders the farmer's real-life warty nose without improvement or idealization. But if the humble farmer poses too self-consciously or dramatically, in a way that he will never quite be found to do in life, we are not likely to hold it against the portrait's realism; just as, though in life he is not centered, framed, and mounted, or cut off at the shoulders, those elements of the picture do not offend our sense of verisimilitude. The reason is that they have been "selected out," overlooked by us in our trained selection of realistic details. However, the realist artist, painter or writer is less easily trained than the rest of us, and so is less easily satisfied by the portrait's partial and selective realism. I will argue in the following pages—it is what I hope the inclusion of Charles Dickens in the company of realists will show—that the realist resents the unreality of the conventions of artistic presentation, such as the posture, the limitation at the edge of the canvas, and the alien frame; and that his resentment has consequences for his art. The principal consequence is the realist's own peculiar use of artistic form. There is a relation of form to content that is just as characteristic and definitive of realism as, in other contexts, a particular subject matter or way of treating visual details might be said to be. To perceive realism's distinctive formal character, we must first comprehend the realist's frustration at the necessary failure of all artistic representation of reality; and then we must learn to recognize those distinctive gestures by which the realist signifies, with only partial coherence but with great longing, the world that lies beyond the farthest border of his power to portray.

1. Form in the Realist Novel:
War and Peace and
Our Mutual Friend

In the opening pages of *War and Peace*, Tolstoy sets before the reader an image of the elite world of St. Petersburg society that is gathered at Anna Schérer's soirée.[1] Perhaps "image" is too monistic a word for what is, in the text, a busy and colorful scene, swarming with vivid particulars, varying details of behavior and appearance, style and intention among the characters; but it is useful here if it calls attention to the impression of wholeness that obtains in the first chapter, in the peculiar consistency and integrity of its details. The image they comprise is one of a closed aristocratic circle, a world in itself, complacent and self-contained. Its effect is to heighten our sense of a world violated, broken in upon, when Pierre Bezhúkhov arrives with his poor manners and questionable social standing. It is upon some of the implications of this wholeness, and of the moment of violation or intrusion, that the next few pages will concentrate.

By what means, first of all, is the image of a closed world conveyed? The mode of the first chapter is, in general, satire. Its target is affectation: "She was, as she said, suffering from *la grippe; la grippe,* being then a new word in St. Petersburg, used only by the elite." The sharpest thrusts are reserved for affectations of sensibility or moral feeling, as in the opening paragraph:

> "Well, Prince, so Genoa and Lucca are now just family estates of the Buonapartes. But I warn you, if you don't tell me that this means war, if you still try to defend the infamies and horrors perpetrated by that Antichrist—I really believe he is Antichrist—I will have nothing to do with you and you are no longer my friend, no longer my 'faithful slave' as you call yourself! But how do you do? I see I have frightened you—sit down and tell me all the news." (I, i, 3)

Here, as throughout the conversation between Anna Schérer and Prince Vasíli Kurágin, the speaker's moral indignation about the overwhelmingly serious political issues of the day is exposed as pretense by the juxtaposition of frivolous and insincere social banter. Of course, the characters are not without their private purposes, about which their feeling is genuine, and then the affectation is of indifference: " 'But tell me,' he added with studied carelessness as if it had only just occurred to him, though the question he was about to ask was the chief motive of his visit . . ." (I, i, 5). In his mask of boredom and languor, the Prince, "like a woundup clock, by force of habit said things he did not even wish to be believed," while Anna Schérer pretends to an enthusiasm and impetuosity, which she affects "sometimes even when she did not feel like it . . . in order not to disappoint the expectations of those who knew her" (I, i, 4). They perform in their opposite but complementary roles with the lifeless uniformity and repetitiveness of robots, a quality shared by nearly everyone at the reception, with the principal (and ultimately heroic) exceptions of Pierre and Prince Andrew. This quality of behavior, in fact, is part of Tolstoy's underlying analogy between conventional social intercourse in this kind of society and the internal functioning of a machine or, alternately, a factory.[2] Here is his description of Anna Schérer's activity when the evening is in full swing:

As the foreman of a spinning mill, when he has set the hands to work, goes round and notices here a spindle that has stopped, or there one that creaks or makes more noise than it should, and hastens to check the machine or set it in proper motion, so Anna Pávlovna moved about her drawing room, approaching now a silent, now a too-noisy group, and by a word or slight rearrangement kept the conversational machine in steady, proper, and regular motion.   (I, i, 10)

The internal functioning of the "conversational machine" is elaborated in another way in the round of favor-seeking and -getting that operates in the room. Kurágin has come in order to ask his hostess' aid in obtaining a diplomatic appointment for his son Anatole. Though she must disappoint him in this, she offers instead to help marry Anatole to a wealthy princess, the sister of Prince Andrew. To do this she must seek the aid of Andrew's wife. Prince Vasíli is gratified, but before he can depart the circle of solicitation must be completed. He is approached by Princess Drubetskáya, whose chief motive in coming to St. Petersburg has been to ask the

Prince's help in obtaining an appointment for *her* son. This circularity, and the reflexive coordination of the whole, as reinforced by numerous details, suggest analogy with closed systems of other kinds: with organic cycles, or artificial systems like games or—particularly relevant in this context—the implicit structure of diplomatic or economic activity. Kurágin actually shows some awareness that he is operating within such a system in his calculation and reflection over Princess Drubetskáya's request: "Influence in society . . . is capital which has to be economized if it is to last. Prince Vasíli knew this, and having once realized that if he asked on behalf of all who begged of him, he would soon be unable to ask for himself, he became chary of using his influence" (I, i, 16).

The analogies with machine and system combine, finally, in a suggestion of a self-determining, autonomously functioning whole. Whatever is fed into the system—court gossip, foreign affairs, or the ideas of that "profound thinker," the Abbé Morio—is ultimately rendered into one uniform fabric. Whatever the input, the process and the output remain autonomous, in point of relevance to or significance for anything outside the system itself. What lies outside the system, what lies beyond the small, elite world, is of course the larger world, of which the other is really a part. And it is the insularity of the smaller world in relation to the greater that Tolstoy's presentation stresses. The contrast is present in the first paragraph of the novel. In fact, it is present in a special and pointed way in the very first sentence: "Well, Prince, so Genoa and Lucca are now just family estates of the Buonapartes." By her metaphor, Anna Schérer accuses Napoleon of converting great public entities into private property. Ironically, she imitates Napoleon's usurpations on the conversational level by making her statement of pretended moral concern the basis of her inane flirtatiousness with the Prince. "Heavens! what a virulent attack!" he replies, converting in a similar way the language of war into (dead) metaphor for the convenience of his wit. In this manner, and by both parties, the external event is annexed, levelled, emptied of its claims to moral seriousness, and woven into that damnably consistent cloth of social frippery against which Tolstoy's judgment is so unmistakable and firm.

This judgment is not without its irony, however. For the way Anna Schérer and Kurágin convert Napoleonic material to their conversational purposes has at least some resemblance to the way Tolstoy makes use of the same material in the novel he is writing. If the former is more openly reductive and irresponsible, there is nonetheless distinctly an element of reduction in the transformation historical fact undergoes when it is adapted to the design of a historical novel. Consider what Napoleon, the concept if not the man, suffers at the hands of Tolstoy and Stendhal. He is demoted from a real, historical person to a character among other characters in a fiction. The novelists trot him out into the field at will, the better to illustrate the heroic visions of their own Nicholas Rostóv and Fabrizio. He is an external fact to be annexed, adapted, and issued forth as part of the uniform fabric of the text. The reductive aspect of this can easily be overstated—especially for *War and Peace*, a novel which urges upon us, around its own edges, as it were, the historicity and actuality of the historical things it contains—but it is certainly there. Our reservation must be that Tolstoy's designs on such material are higher, more valuable, than

Anna Schérer's, which are, as Prince Andrew would say, all vanity. It is rather the structure of their discourse that is analogous.

The first implication of the analogy between the assimilation process of the novel and that of the closed world or system Tolstoy has described is that the novel, too, is a closed world or system of some kind; and this is arguably true of all novels, if only in respect of *form*. To say so has at least the minimal soundness of tautology. Form is closure. To shape is to exclude the surrounding world. And it is chiefly through the element of form, as I have already said, that criticism of the last few decades has taught us to apprehend the essence of a literary work. We show the impact of formalism on our reading of novels when, in speaking of the "world of a novel," or even of a novelist, we mean not the world within which the novel exists, but the world that exists within it. We do not mean that the novel cannot or does not resemble, refer to, or even attempt to describe the real, outlying world, but that, when it does so, such reference is automatically converted into the stuff of the novel's own making. "Instead of dichotomizing 'form-content'," say Wellek and Warren, "we should think of matter and then of 'form,' that which aesthetically organizes its 'matter.' In a successful work of art, the materials are completely assimilated into the form: what was 'world' has become 'language'."[3]

Formalism's emphasis when dealing with the historical or realist novel is usually on the thoroughness of this assimilation:

The centre of literary art is obviously to be found in the traditional genres of the lyric, the epic, the drama. In all of them, the reference is to a world of fiction, of imagination.

The statements in a novel, in a poem, or in a drama are not
literally true; they are not logical propositions. There is a
central and important difference between a statement, even in
a historical novel or a novel by Balzac which seems to convey
"information" about actual happenings, and the same
information appearing in a book of history or sociology.[4]

In this view, it is only the cohering, formal whole that is
capable of "correspondence" to the real world. Particulars
within the novel can register their significance for the
outer world only indirectly, by their atomic modification
of the whole.[5] "The theory of realism is ultimately bad
aesthetics because all art is 'making,' and is a world in itself of illusion and symbolic forms."[6] It is by virtue of
their closure, then, that novels are what they are, and say
what they have to say.

A generation after its first systematic expression, this
argument has acquired a ring of orthodoxy. If its emphasis is sufficient as well as necessary, it makes nonsense of
my earlier reservation that it is only the form of novels
that is to be regarded as closed. What is there other than
form that I would leave somehow open? Or rather—
because the distinction between form and content can
always be made at least theoretically—what is there
somehow "in" a novel other than what finds expression
in the novel's (closed) form? And to the force of this
question must be added the force of the evaluative corollary of the formalist position, that it is only in less than
"successful" novels that assimilation is incomplete, and
some trace of "world" is left upon the language. My hint
that novels can have an open, unenclosed aspect would
be true, in that case, only for bad novels.

Is it true for *War and Peace?* We have seen that Wellek and Warren make forthright mention of the historical novel "or a novel by Balzac" despite the considerable complications of their theory of assimilation these inclusions entail. But perhaps, as Frank Brady notes, they do not do so without betraying a certain "uneasiness" in their prose, and uneasiness is probably warranted.[7] Here are two "statements" from *War and Peace:*

(1) As the Tsar, rode up to one flank of the battalions, which presented arms, another group of horsemen galloped up to the opposite flank, and at the head of them Rostóv recognized Napoleon.   (v, xviii, 449)

(2) Napoleon began the war with Russia because he could not resist going to Dresden, could not help having his head turned by the homage he received, could not help donning a Polish uniform and yielding to the stimulating influence of a June morning, and could not refrain from bursts of anger in the presence of Kurákin and then of Balashëv.   (x, i, 761)

These sentences have in common that power to signify which formalism recognizes in the contribution of any particular to our understanding of the novel as a totality. Rostóv's glimpse of Napoleon at the Peace of Tilsit in (1) has arguably a rather crucial function in this respect, and (2) is from one of Tolstoy's direct disquisitions on historical matters which, as critics have increasingly acknowledged, relate in complex and telling ways to the themes and action of the novel on the fictive level.[8] But there is at the same time a solid, ontological difference between the statements, for which formalism can offer no good account: that (2), whatever its "coherential" significance, has also the capacity to mean what it says outside the novel. Its contingency is relatively less than that of (1), there is relatively more "world" clinging to it, despite its assimilation. And there can be no condition of reader- ship so pure as to be oblivious of this difference, or unaf- fected by it. Our awareness of a potential autonomy or "escape" from the text in (2) inevitably affects our re- sponse to (1). Under its influence, we return to Rostóv at Tilsit, this time not so much for what the scene shows us about Rostóv, as for what the fictive idea of Nicholas Ros- tóv may tell us about the historical subject itself. By this effect, the claim of actuality, of historicity, is sustained outside the purely discursive chapters, even in that bulk of the book where the real and the imaginary mingle.

Of course, it is always possible, and a great deal simpler, to condemn as excrescences such passages as (2), and critics of various persuasions have not hesitated to do so. No doubt it was in the plenitude of (2), with its disturbing effect on (1), that Henry James located the looseness and bagginess of the monster.[9] Nonetheless, the effect I am describing can be considered one of the central and distinguishing features of the historical novel—and also, perhaps, of the realist, for what is true of a statement by Tolstoy about Napoleon may well be true of a statement by Balzac about the provincial clergy, or by Dickens about the Poor Law. And the failure of a critical approach to account for it says more about the limitations of the approach than about the aesthetics of the novelist.

We know that Tolstoy, who was never very pleasant on the subject of literary criticism, had an especially keen dislike for the very idea of the "novel form."[10] He repeat- edly denied that *War and Peace* was a novel at all, not because of its didacticism, but because of what he regarded, significantly, as its shapelessness. In a discarded preface to the first volume he wrote:

In publishing the beginning of my projected work, I do not promise a continuation or conclusion. We Russians generally speaking do not know how to write novels in the sense in which this genre is understood in Europe, nor is the projected work a long short story; no single idea runs through it, no contention is made, no single event is described; still less can it be called a novel with a plot, with a constantly deepening interest, and with a happy or unhappy denouement destroying the interest of the narrative.[11]

This passage quivers with resistance to formal restraints and closure of any kind. We have already seen what is probably the consequence for the novel of this disposition in its creator: that the approach to novels as closed worlds is one particularly ill-suited to the study of *War and Peace*. But if this is so, what is the significance of the analogy so readily available in the opening scene, between the closed world of the nobility and the enterprise of Tolstoy's novel? For the answer we must return to Anna Schérer's soirée:

One of the next arrivals was a stout, heavily built young man with close-cropped hair, spectacles, the light-colored breeches fashionable at that time, a very high ruffle, and a brown dress coat. This stout young man was an illegitimate son of Count Bezhúkhov, a well-known grandee of Catherine's time who now lay dying in Moscow. The young man had not yet entered either the military or civil service, as he had only just returned from abroad where he had been educated, and this was his first appearance in society. Anna Pávlovna greeted him with the nod she accorded to the lowest hierarchy in her drawing room. But in spite of this lowest-grade greeting, a look of anxiety and fear, as at the sight of something too large and unsuited to the place, came over her face when she saw

Pierre enter. Though he was certainly rather bigger than the
other men in the room, her anxiety could only have reference
to the clever though shy, but observant and natural,
expression which distinguished him from everyone else in that
drawing room.

"It is very good of you, Monsieur Pierre, to come and visit
a poor invalid," said Anna Pávlovna, exchanging an alarmed
glance with her aunt as she conducted him to her.

Pierre murmured something unintelligible, and continued
to look round as if in search of something.   (I, i, 9)

Critics responding to this passage have sometimes sin-
gled out the attribution to Pierre of a "natural expression," which contrasts with the affectations of the other
guests. This is important, but there may be something of
hindsight in the emphasis. Tolstoy's young hero is presented to us, first of all, through the eyes of a relatively
minor character—a favorite device of the author's—and,
because of Anna Schérer's preoccupation, it is the new
guest's clumsiness and *gaucherie* of which we are first
made aware.[12] He is a monkey-wrench tossed into the
works of the social machine she is carefully tending: an
"illegitimate" member of society, "too large and unsuited" for assimilation, "unintelligible" by the operative
code. "Educate this bear for me!" says Prince Vasíli to his
hostess, using a figure that combines Pierre's naturalness
and his clumsiness. Now the bear in the popular imagination is not only a clumsy animal, but also a dangerous
one. Thus Pierre's repeated improprieties and general in-
elegance are largely comic, even rather charming in the
eyes of the guests; but to the gravest of his *faux pas*, his
defence of Napoleon as the greatest man of the age, their
response, if only for a moment, is one of genuine alarm.

What the arrival of the large young man and the disturbance he causes suggest about the form of the novel would already be obvious if his advocacy of Napoleon did not make it more so. Pierre the unassimilable alien stands in relation to the polite assembly as the novel's own sprawling, heroic subject matter stands toward the conventional novel form. But inevitably, and if only in some partial, partially shattered way, conventional novel form is the form of *War and Peace.* The resulting spectacle is that of a great novel, mightily, purposefully, at variance with its own form.

The main thrust of this may be turned aside in two ways. Despite Tolstoy's disclaimer, *War and Peace* is held together on one level by a conventional though more than usually complex inter-development of plot, character, setting, theme. The St. Petersburg drawing room intrigues; Pierre's own systematic self-consciousness throughout his long middle period; the precisely telling parallels among individuals and families, marriages and careers—these expressions of the activity and creativity of human consciousness within the novel may be taken to mirror the novelist's own stance toward the raw historical-experiential data he is organizing. It is open to us to read the novel wholly on this level, while deprecating, like James, all the rest as *longueurs* and digressions. But this is willfully to ignore how these delicate, reflexive structures are swept away in the novel, again and again, by the external, impersonal force of history, the irresistible and literally historical reality of the Napoleonic invasion. *War and Peace* is so challenging to the notion of novels as games or systems, because in it the pieces are periodically scattered, knocked off the board; and no sooner are they gathered up again, and play resumed, than the devastation is repeated. The course of play in such a game would be nothing short of bizarre if it were not, as it happens, richly suggestive. The repeated devastations themselves become a metaphor, of which Pierre's entrance is a preliminary exemplum, for the vulnerability of any creation of human consciousness—a marriage, a novel, a theory of history—to the disordering impact of actuality. All closure is artificial. All formal creations must surrender to the press of the actual at their borders or wither in their isolation and irrelevance.

Of course, it is easier to advocate openness in a novel, by metaphor or critical declamation, than to achieve such a thing as open form.[13] In my brief comparison of the two selected sentences from the novel, I tried to show how the potentially independent, relatively less contingent passages in a text can have a liberating effect on the more strictly contingent, the "purely fictive." That demonstration is still incomplete, and it now becomes important to add that the effect is reversible. That is, we cannot be oblivious to the reductive, de-actualizing effect of the fictional context, the novel form, on the direct historical discourse. This realization gives rise to a second way of resisting Tolstoy's anti-formal emphasis, which is to argue from the very inexorability of his dependence on form. Tolstoy may try to represent the sprawling and the formless by the intrusion of chaos upon a formal whole, but, the argument goes, in doing so he will merely create a new formal whole. To incorporate the disruption of form by the apparently formless is, after all, only to create new form; to represent the apparently formless is, after all, only to give it apparent form. The necessary limits of his medium may seem to Tolstoy a cruel confinement, but his rage against them, from this point of view, is a misguided and ill-tempered quarrel with the facts of artistic creation—"bad aesthetics," as Wellek has already told us.

The sophistry of this argument rests upon a complacent equation of form to content in works of art. There are two things to say about this equation. The first is that it has disabling consequences for critical practice. By its light, we cannot distinguish between two orders of artistic performance: between those works which have their meaning in an obedience to form—a scrupulous or subtle or easeful fulfilment of formal exigencies, as in a sonnet, or a story by de Maupassant—and those which sacrifice form for vision, when necessary. Works of the latter class, to which the realist novels of the nineteenth century emphatically belong, allow themselves to be pushed out of shape from within, as it were, by the excessive weight or incongruous outline of their creative burdens— one thinks of the poetry of Whitman, the unshapely explosions of Turner, the massive ideational indulgences of Dostoyevsky.

A criticism which cannot distinguish de Mapaussant's use of form from Dostoyevsky's is, of course, singularly incompetent. Beyond its incompetence, however, we must take note of its perversity. There is something willful and self-blinding, surely, about the critic's refusal to see the artist's evident intention (to represent formlessness) simply because the complete realization of the intention is impossible (because of the tautology of form). In fact, though, the real basis for this refusal is not so theoretical. It is, rather, the fear of being led away from the security of artistic closure, of being led back to the world's uncertainty from the formally guaranteed certainties of the work of art. Such a gesture as Tolstoy's creation of Pierre directs the reader's attention towards an expanse of things surrounding the novel but not included in it, a horizon that stretches away from the work of art, illimitable and in all directions: the horizon, perhaps, which Flora Finching names, in *Little Dorrit*, the "horizon of etcetera." The critic we have been describing, however responsive he may be to the inward suggestiveness of the writing, however sensitive to its features in themselves, nonetheless refuses to turn his eyes upon that reality which the work of art itself invokes, describes, engages. In a narrow sense, he fails the text, as a reader; beyond that, he fails the text's intended community of creation, conversation, response.

But a narrower version of creativity is more familiar and influential. "With its greatest writers, with Balzac and Dickens, Dostoyevsky and Tolstoy," writes Wellek, realism "constantly went beyond its theory: it created worlds of imagination." [14] The widely echoed implication is that the theory of realism was itself by no means conducive to great art; that the historical-realist project in nineteenth-century fiction, which was to describe the real world instead of or in addition to creating an imaginary one, was unliterary—not so much an impossible ideal as an error in taste and judgment. But certain realist artists, unconsciously, as it were, and accidentally, eluded the onus of representational achievement, and presented ordered, fictive wholes, in spite of themselves.

In fact, however, once the true nature of realism in relation to its form has been grasped, there is no reason to restrict ourselves to so implicitly condescending an admiration of realist masterworks. The success of realism reveals itself in the paradox—or the marvel or the absurdity—of a novel that tells us of real things and imaginary things, alternately and together, sometimes without discernible shift in mode; and yet assumes, in doing so, that it will not impair its credibility on either the real or the fictive level. We may choose to attend only to one-half of the novel, or to argue aesthetics with the whole. Neither response is satisfactory; both are lacking, simply, in innocence. Perhaps Wellek is right in saying that the theory of realism is bad aesthetics; but it is clear, too, on the strength of the foregoing discussion of *War and Peace*, that it is in their conflict with their own imperfect aesthetic ideals that the masterpieces of realism have their meaning. And if that is so, we are at a grave disadvantage if we cannot posit such a thing as a conflict between content and form. For novels are like people, and will not reveal their inner conflicts to those who do not have the means to be sympathetic.

2

"When, for instance, we pick up a novel of Dickens," according to Northrop Frye,

our immediate impulse, a habit fostered in us by all the criticism we know, is to compare it with "life," whether as lived by us or by Dickens' contemporaries. Then we meet such characters as Heep or Quilp, and, as neither we nor the Victorians have ever known anything much "like" these curious monsters, the method promptly breaks down. Some

readers will complain that Dickens has relapsed into "mere"
caricature . . . ; others, more sensibly, simply give up the
criterion of lifelikeness and enjoy the creation for its own
sake.[15]

I do not cite this fragment of argument from Northrop
Frye's *Anatomy of Criticism* because the case it makes is so
convincing. Its strategies of punctuation—"life" is a du-
bious entity, requiring quotation marks that "the creation for its own sake" can do without—hint openly at
how the logic can be undone. There are many ways of
being "like" Quilp or Heep, all of them familiar; and
Heep, by the way, is surely of a different order of plausi-
bility than the rapacious dwarf, with his much apparent
fairy-tale ancestry. Of course, neither Heep nor Quilp is
"normal," a word which should always be in quotation
marks, and it is the "normal" that Frye makes, in effect,
the standard of what is lifelike. Others, more sensibly,
would allow the latter a wider connotation. Quilps and
Heeps and Gamps and Squeerses do indeed differ from
human beings as we know them, but, on one level, only
as some human beings differ from most others. More
often than is commonly admitted, Dickens' "exaggera-
tions" are faithful imitations of reality's own exaggerated
specimens. This response, moreover, is one that Dickens
himself was wont to make to accusations like Frye's. "I
find," he wrote, "that a great many people (particularly
those who might have sat for the character) consider even
Mr. Pecksniff a grotesque impossibility, and Mrs. Nickleby herself, sitting bodily before me in a solid chair,
once asked me whether I believed there ever was such a
woman."[16] Or, less satirically, in the Preface to *Martin
Chuzzlewit:*

What is exaggeration to one class of minds . . . is plain truth
to another . . . I sometimes ask myself whether there may
occasionally be a difference of this kind between some writers
and some readers; whether it is *always* the writer who colours
highly, or whether it is now and then the reader whose eye for
colour is a little dull?[17]

Frye recognizes, of course, the high color of Dickens' creation; his eye for color is very good indeed. But he does
not see that what is colorful and vivid in Dickens has a
mimetic base as well as a literary tradition (in the "theory
of humours"); it has a basis in reality that Frye, like most
readers of the literary creation "for its own sake," is un-
willing to recognize.[18]

 Frye's views are given as an example of a "normal"
response to the question of Dickens' realism rather than a
tenable one—and realism, by the way, is another term
Frye holds in brisk contempt.[19] His remarks are of special
interest here because, as a more generous show of context would make clear,they dissent from a (loosely) mimetic standard on grounds that cannot be called formalis-
tic. Moreover, the passage from Frye illustrates what in
part it means to say: "Lifelikeness" is a shifty and irresponsible criterion, so shifty in fact that it is just as likely
to do damage to the arguments of those who repudiate its
use as to the arguments of those who use it. Admittedly
it is a word imperfect in its connotation, but how and
when it can be put to rest is a question that requires investigation of the other and more complex word, mimesis, of which such terms as "lifelikeness," verisimilitude,
and realism itself are variously rich and poor relations.
And of mimesis Dickens offers a relevant parable in the
second chapter of *Our Mutual Friend:*

The great looking-glass above the sideboard, reflects the table and the company. Reflects the new Veneering crest, in gold and eke in silver, frosted and also thawed, a camel of all work. . . . Reflects Veneering; forty, wavy-haired, tending to corpulence, sly, mysterious, filmy—a kind of sufficiently well-looking veiled-prophet, not prophesying. Reflects Mrs Veneering; fair, aquiline-nosed and fingered, not so much light hair as she might have, gorgeous in raiment and jewels, enthusiastic, propitiatory, conscious that a corner of her husband's veil is over herself. Reflects Podsnap; prosperously feeding, two little light-coloured wiry wings, one on either side of his else bald head, looking as like his hairbrushes as his hair, dissolving view of red beads on his forehead, large allowance of crumpled shirtcollar up behind. Reflects Mrs Podsnap; . . . quantity of bone, neck and nostrils like a rockinghorse, hard features, majestic head-dress in which Podsnap has hung golden offerings. Reflects Twemlow; grey, dry, polite, susceptible to east wind, First-Gentleman-in-Europe collar and cravat, cheeks drawn in as if he had made a great effort to retire into himself some years ago, and had got so far and had never got any farther. Reflects mature young lady; raven locks, and complexion that lights up well when well powdered—as it is—carrying on considerably in the captivation of mature young gentleman; with too much nose in his face, too much ginger in his whiskers, too much torso in his waistcoat, too much sparkle in his studs, his eyes, his buttons, his talk, and his teeth. Reflects charming Lady Tippins on Veneering's right; with an immense obtuse drab oblong face, like a face in a tablespoon . . . Reflects a certain 'Mortimer,' another of Veneering's oldest friends; who never was in the house before, and appears not to want to come again, who sits disconsolate on Mrs Veneering's left, and who was inveigled by Lady Tippins (a friend of his boyhood) to come to these people's and talk, and who won't talk. Reflects Eugene, friend of Mortimer; buried alive in the back of his chair, behind a shoulder—with a powder-epaulette on it—of the mature young lady, and gloomily resorting to the champagne chalice whenever proffered by the Analytical

Chemist. Lastly the looking-glass reflects Boots and Brewer, and two other stuffed Buffers interposed between the rest of the company and possible accidents.   (I, ii, 52–53)

Apparently Dickens is delighted with his "great looking glass" and takes the opportunity of showing us all the great variety of things he can do with visual details in a fictional tableau. In the portrait of Podsnap, for example, the "two little light-coloured wiry wings" which are "as like his hairbrushes as his hair" contribute to a fuller visual image, but they also suggest something about the stiffness of the man—whereas the "dissolving view of red beads on his forehead" looks back to the "stickey" [sic] surface of the Veneerings' furniture as well as carrying a strong suggestion of heated pent-up-ness, a quality of repression that will later be elaborately confirmed. His sweat is further related to the symbolic continuum of water and liquids generally so often remarked in the novel—for example, the river and blood in Chapter One, the "poisoned" chablis and champagne in Chapter Two—just as the "raven locks" of the "mature young lady" may have something to do with "birds of prey," the novel's image for the corpse-robbers in Chapter One. Sweat, moreover, is repeatedly associated with Podsnap later on, as in the "mutton vapour-bath" of a dinner party he gives in Chapter Eleven, which is followed by a chapter about Rogue Riderhood called "The Sweat of an Honest Man's Brow." And as sweat is to Podsnap, the "rocking-horse" image is to his wife, and an excess of sparkle is to Lammle. Another use of visual particulars is demonstrated in the detail that Twemlow wears a "First-Gentleman-in-Europe" collar and cravat, which, in addition to suggesting something picturesque and archaic about the little man, is also a foreshadowing of a more important matter: Twemlow will eventually prove the true gentleman of this circle by his response to Wrayburn's marriage. His attitude on that occasion will compare to the attitude of those around him as his quaint style of collar compares here to Podsnap's "large allowance of shirt-collar crumpled up behind." A similar thematic hint is contained in the depiction of the slouching Eugene as "buried alive" on the outskirts of the dinner party.

The task of presenting to us what the mirror reflects greatly exercises Dickens' powers of description, although what results has an air of effortlessness about it, and gives numerous opportunities for the highly figurative Dickensian romp of language: simile, metaphor, synecdoche, hyperbole. The quintessential Dickensian flavor which attaches to this passage is a product, in equal and inextricable parts, of figurative language, an almost disembodied satiric stance, and an immediate and not entirely accountable vivacity and "lifelikeness" in the characters. No less characteristic of the writer is the device itself, the suspended mirror that frames the scene of the novel's preliminary exposition of plot and characters, and "Reflects . . . Reflects . . . Reflects." The mirror that reflects and frames has its counterpart in *Little Dorrit* in the sun that stares and imprisons, and in *Bleak House* in the fog that circles and ensnares. The frame holds for the remainder of the chapter, by which time Mortimer has acquainted the reader with the Harmon story, and even the Boffins and Bella Wilfer have at least been mentioned. It is easy to see why G. K. Chesterton said that this scene was "of course" the beginning of the novel.[20] Added to what is reflected in the mirror, Mortimer's story places a significant portion of the "world" of the novel before us.

One possible way of taking this capacious mirror is indicated by the subject-ellipsis of "Reflects . . ." which suggests the transparency and even the absence of the reflecting medium.[21] Syntactically the glass disappears but the reflection remains. Thus the mirror is what it reflects, which at its furthest reach is very nearly the novel itself. Now the idea of the novel as mirror carries a considerable weight of literary-historical and -theoretical suggestion. There is reason to suspect that the mirror hanging in the Veneering's dining room formerly belonged to Stendhal, who kept it in the roadway. It is, in other words, the simplest and most honored of the emblems of art as mimesis, held up, for this narrative moment, not to Nature but to Society.

Except that it is not quite true that the entire world of the novel is reflected in the glass. Mortimer produces the Harmons, the Boffins, and Bella out of himself, as it were, or from within that which the mirror already contains. But before he is done, he is interrupted by the arrival of a note from Charley Hexam, who is a representative of the novel's lower world, the world of Gaffer Hexam and Bradley Headstone, as the boy's axial relation to those men makes clear. Unlike Mortimer's story, which it brings to a putative conclusion, the note constitutes an intrusion *ab extra* on the world of the mirror, from how alien an environment Mortimer and Eugene will shortly discover, on their journey to Southwark. Says Mortimer, when he has read the note, "the story is completer . . . than I supposed." But in fact, of course, the story has hardly begun. Its completeness is an illusion like the illusion of completeness in the mirror itself, the illusion that the world of the novel is or can be self-limited and entire within its frame. It is this illusion that is abruptly exposed by Charley's communication. The frame is shattered by it, and story and chapter are over at once. The news which does the damage is the supposed drowning of John Harmon, and it is in this unguessable, unsociable, and actually violent piece of untruth, rather than in the mounting of the great mimetic frame, that the novel has its real beginning.

It appears from this that whatever use Dickens is making of the mirror as an emblem of the mimetic art of his novel is ambivalent and doubtful. That he delights in exploiting it we have already seen; but the intrusion upon the closed world of the mirror is an effect equally dramatic and grand, and urges, in the opposite direction, the mirror's inadequacy as a symbol of representational art.

It will help us in this quandary to note that the use of the mirror is related to the chapter's preoccupation with surfaces, with shine, polish, powder, and varnish, with veil and veneer:

> For, in the Veneering establishment, from the hall-chairs with the new coat of arms, to the grand piano-forte with the new action, and upstairs again to the new fire-escape, all things were in a state of high varnish and polish. And what was observable in the furniture, was observable in the Veneerings—the surface smelt a little too much of the workshop, and was a trifle stickey.   (I, ii, 48)

As this example shows, the preoccupation with surface is other than neutral: Surface, or rather a world that seems indeed to be all surface, is both satirized and unsmilingly disdained. But significantly it is about the surfaces of things that mirrors most nearly tell the truth. Mirrors "lie," as it were, in two places: at their edges, and in their denial of the third dimension, their inherent denial of depth. Charley's intrusion actually points up both these limitations, the lack of depth as well as the exclusion at the borders of the representation. He comes, as I have said, from the novel's underworld, a term which in itself suggests what the novel will seek at length to demonstrate about depths and surfaces in society: that the superficial world of new and false gentility is supported from beneath, in reality, by a world of mud, filth, and decay, instinctual and violent and pervaded by death. The two worlds are really one world, of which the mirror only presents the glittering surface of a restricted area. The very notion of a distance between the two worlds is, in effect, a false insinuation of the mirror itself, which draws up arbitrary borders, and claims to represent reality when it can only represent the surfaces of things. Something similar, moreover, about the treachery of surfaces is implied in the idea of a man drowning, an implication which is furthered much later, when, in Headstone's attack on Wrayburn, the river is compared to a mirror (iv, vi, 766–67).

The lies and illusions fostered by the mirror in its very nature become more important as they are seen to be expressive of attitudes toward reality held by members of the Veneering circle. This point is apparent in the comedy of mistaken identities that follows Podsnap's arrival. Relationships among the characters are so superficial that Podsnap does not know his host when he enters, but a few minutes later is named Godfather to the

new Veneering. Momentarily, Veneering resents Podsnap's mistaking of Twemlow for himself, and the terms
of his resentment are interesting: "It is questionable
whether any man quite relishes being mistaken for any
other man; but, Mr Veneering having this very evening
set up the shirt-front of the young Antinous in new
worked cambric just come home, is not at all compli-
mented by being supposed to be Twemlow, who is dry
and weazen and some thirty years older" (I, ii, 50–51).

The mistaking of identities here is the mistaking of
the surface of one man for the surface of another. Veneering, however, feels the slight not to his inner self, but to
his "shirtfront." He resents that his surface has been
mistaken for that of a man who really has a different and,
to his mind, inferior surface. This differs from Twemlow's offense at the same mistake in a signal way: "As to
Twemlow, he is so sensible of being a much better bred
man than Veneering that he considers the large man an
offensive ass." Twemlow's superiority to the company,
which will later make itself apparent, is here fore-
shadowed by his consulting an other than superficial
standard of identity, the snobbery of "better bred" notwithstanding.

Some implications of this are furthered in Chapter
Eleven, "Podsnappery." There we learn that Podsnap
"was well to do, and stood very high in Mr Podsnap's
opinion," having "thriven exceedingly in the Marine In-
surance way." His business, it is interesting to observe,
depends for its success on keeping things on the surface.
But the parallel with mirrors actually goes much further:

Thus happily acquainted with his own merit and
importance, Mr Podsnap settled that whatever he put behind
him he put out of existence. There was a dignified

conclusiveness—not to add a grand convenience—in this way
of getting rid of disagreeables which had done much towards
establishing Mr Podsnap in his lofty place in Mr Podsnap's
satisfaction. "I don't want to know about it; I don't choose to
discuss it; I don't admit it!" Mr Podsnap had even acquired a
peculiar flourish of his right arm in often clearing the world of
its most difficult problems, by sweeping them behind him
(and consequently sheer away) with those words and a flushed
face. For they affronted him.   (I, xi, 174)

Podsnap's conception of reality, like the mirror's, "admits" only what is before it, not what is behind it, and
then only within certain bounds. What is stressed above
is the insularity and complacency of such a conception,
and these qualities are surely not absent from the Veneerings' table. But that the narrowness and flatness of
conception shared by Podsnap and the mirror have direct
reference to the idea of art as representation is manifest
in what follows. After noting, Q. E. D., that Mr. Podsnap's "world was not a very large world," Dickens cites
as an illustration Podsnap's "notions of the Arts." Literature, painting, sculpture, and even music are required by
Podsnap's aesthetic to be "respectfully" and "sedately
expressive of getting up at eight, shaving close at a
quarter past, breakfasting at nine, going to the City at
ten, coming home at half-past five, and dining at seven.
Nothing else to be permitted to those same vagrants the
Arts, on pain of excommunication. Nothing else To Be—
anywhere!" (I, xi, 175).

The logic in the sequence of these passages, furthermore, shows how to a Podsnappish mind epistemology
dictates aesthetics in a very direct and simple way, which
Dickens seems to have found ludicrous. Podsnap's conception of what makes up the real world is restricted to
the visible exterior of the mid-Victorian life of London as

it was lived, it may be said without cant, by the purest
strain of the bourgeoisie; and within these bounds is all
the reality that art may imitate. What is ugly, what is offensive, what is unsuited on moral grounds for the ears
of "the young person," is of course ruled out, but avow-
edly on the grounds that it is unreal: "I don't admit it!"
Such Philistinism may seem so overdrawn as to have
only the narrowest applicability; although, as we have
seen, it is possible for a critic with the erudition of a
Northrop Frye to assume that mimetic critics must, like
Podsnap, necessarily equate what is real ("lifelike"?)
with what is normal in our daily experience ("our" daily
experience). In fact, though, Frye's assumption of our
narrowness proves quite pertinent to the case of one
famous critic of this novel. In his review, the young
Henry James decided it was the "poorest" of Dickens' ef-
forts, for reasons like the following:

In former days there reigned in Mr. Dickens' extravagances a
comparative consistency; they were exaggerated statements of
types that really existed. We had, perhaps, never known a
Newman Noggs, nor a Pecksniff, nor a Micawber; but we had
known persons of whom these figures were but the logical
consummation. But among the grotesque creatures who
occupy the pages before us, there is not one whom we can
refer to as an existing type.[22]

The developmental emphasis of this is irrelevant. Newman Noggs may seem to some readers more "lifelike"
than Mr. Boffin—who particularly offends James—as I
have said that Heep is more plausible than Quilp, but
one cannot build a theory of Dickens' career as a novelist
on such judgments. Rather, the interesting element in the
above is that which culminates in the question James

asks later in his essay: "Who represents nature?"[23] The Marxist critic Arnold Kettle has answered James's question with another: "Whose nature?"[24] Significantly, Kettle's essay is marred by a narrowness of conception at least equal to that which he attributes to the Jamesian idea of "nature"; but he is surely right that James's judgment is disadvantaged by virtue of his class bias. James finds Rogue Riderhood, for example, believable in his literally irredeemable villainy because of the "quarter of society" to which he belongs, but wonders whether such "elegant swindlers" as Fascination Fledgeby and Alfred Lammle would, in the real world, be so "aggressive."[25] Such a delusion deserves to be called Podsnappish. In uncovering it, I am not the first to find something of the Philistine in this most epicurean of novelists.[26]

I have tried to show what the mirror has in common with what Dickens attacks as Podsnappery in order to further the argument that Dickens is making of the mirror a negative paradigm of the novel's art. This is not the place to enter into a defense against the most famous judgment James makes in his review, that Dickens is "the greatest of superficial novelists": "It is one of the chief conditions of his genius not to see beneath the surface of things."[27] But it is a good beginning to see, as we have done, the objections Dickens makes to the means of representation symbolized in *Our Mutual Friend* by the mirror: for one thing, that it does not allow one to see beneath the surface of things. Of course, James is rightly interested in Dickens' performance as a writer, and not in his aesthetic *per se*. But it is at least cautionary to perceive that, in his treatment of the mirror, Dickens is join-

ing in the judgment against superficial representation
that was to become classic when applied to his own case.

Dickens is using the mirror, moreover, as Tolstoy
used the analogy between the novel and the closed social
system at the beginning of *War and Peace*. Mirror and
system are first of all devices for ordering the presentation of the Veneerings' dinner party and Anna Schérer's
soirée, respectively; but both come to have recognizable
implications for the novel and its form. By their nature
they suggest the self-containment and superficiality, the
complacency and exclusivity of the drawing-rooms, and
these qualities in turn have reference to certain mimetic
or representational limits inherent in the mirror-like or
system-like form of a novel. In short, the two novelists
offer the analogies of mirror and system for their craft in
order to smash them, to reject them because of the formal
restraints and closure they imply. There is furthermore
an unmistakable resemblance in the actual incidents by
means of which the restraints are broken down. The language used to describe Charley Hexam when he stands
before Mortimer and Eugene recalls the description of
Tolstoy's dangerous and ultimately ineducable bear:
"There was a curious mixture in the boy, of uncompleted
savagery, and uncompleted civilization" (i, iii, 60). In
both cases, an alien, not wholly assimilable individual
has arrived, who carries in his bearing the proof of how
limited a portion of reality mirror or system can reflect,
organize, absorb, or otherwise contain. But it must be
repeated that the forms so assailed by the novelists are
precisely the forms upon which they must depend for the
expression of content. As the looking-glass passage itself
testifies, it would be the most tendentious absurdity to

deny how large a portion of Dickens' genius resides in his portrayal of surface detail, or in the use of figurative language which surface details occasion; and likewise one cannot easily name a novel more systematic in its way than Tolstoy's giant masterpiece. The damage they inflict by design upon mirror and system as analogues of restricted form is damage inflicted, finally, upon the forms of their own art.

Mortimer Lightwood is a solicitor by profession, and not a narrative artist, but the role of storyteller is forced upon him at the Veneerings' table by the emphatic request of Lady Tippins that he tell the story of the "Man from Somewhere." The guests have been encouraged by Lady Tippins to expect that the story they are about to hear is exciting and exotic, and it is this expectation in his hearers that Mortimer begins by seeking to deflate. But this he is oddly unable to do. "Sorry to destroy romance by fixing him with a local habitation," he says of the Man from Somewhere, "but he comes from the place, the name of which escapes me, but will suggest itself to everybody else here, where they make the wine." The effect of this failure of memory is to leave in the air a little of that sense of mystery Mortimer hopes to dispel by the urbanity and cool wit of his delivery, which is "founded" on that of Eugene. The Man from Somewhere is the son of a wealthy dust contractor named Harmon, and it is of the father Mortimer is speaking:

"The moral being—I believe that's the right expression—of this exemplary person, derived its highest gratification from anathematizing his nearest relations and turning them out of doors. Having begun (as was natural) by rendering these attentions to the wife of his bosom, he next found himself at leisure to bestow a similar recognition on the claims of his daughter. He chose a husband for her, entirely to his own satisfaction and not in the least to hers, and proceeded to settle upon her, as her marriage portion, I don't know how much Dust, but something immense. At this stage of the affair the poor girl respectively intimated that she was secretly engaged to that popular character whom the novelists and versifiers call Another, and that such a marriage would make Dust of her heart and Dust of her life—in short, would set her up, on a very extensive scale, in her father's business. Immediately the venerable parent—on a cold winter's night, it is said—anathematized and turned her out."   (I, ii, 56)

Mortimer's sarcasm, it hardly needs saying, is two-edged. "The moral being—I believe that's the right expression" and "Having begun (as was natural) by rendering these attentions to the wife of his bosom." In these words there is moral judgment, disapprobation of Harmon, but there is also ridicule of the ordinary use of moral language, the cheap currency of talk about what is right and natural. From such talk Mortimer seeks to separate himself by the irony of his style. We know that he is self-conscious of his role as the teller of a story with a mordantly ethical content even before he mocks the "novelists and versifiers" who also tell stories in which "Another" appears. And perhaps it is not irrelevant that the most famous appearance of "Another" in English literature, perhaps, occurs in *Martin Chuzzlewit*, where he is the object of Augustus Moddle's bathetic envy. Mortimer continues:

"The pecuniary resources of Another were, as they usually are, of a very limited nature. I believe I am not using too strong an expression when I say that Another was hard up. However, he married the young lady, and they lived in a humble dwelling,

probably possessing a porch ornamented with honeysuckle
and woodbine twining, until she died. I must refer you to the
Registrar of the District in which the humble dwelling was
situated, for the certified cause of death; but early sorrow and
anxiety may have had something to do with it, though they
may not appear in the ruled pages and printed forms.
Indisputably this was the case with Another, for he was so cut
up by the loss of his young wife that if he outlived her a year
it was as much as he did." (ι, ii, 56–57)

Here Mortimer's *dipsychus* is transparent. There is something greater even than his repugnance for the conventions of the sentimental romance of his era, and that is
his feeling for its mimetic base—his sympathy with the
real-life heroine of such a story, and even with Another
himself. Their fate is recorded in the gift-book romance
as their deaths are certified in the official Register of the
District, and in both cases the essential truth is distorted
or missed. Mortimer mocks the kind of story he must tell
in telling the truth, by means of such verbal incongruities
as "Another was hard up," or in describing the "porch
ornamented with honeysuckle and woodbine twining,"
but the real cause of death, "early sorrow and anxiety," is
given in words whose simplicity and force are greater
than the force of the satire on romance and official Register to which they are juxtaposed. The feeling behind
them is the subject of Dickens' intrusion as narrator:

There is that in the indolent Mortimer, which seems to
hint that if good society might on any account allow itself to
be impressible, he, one of good society, might have the
weakness to be impressed by what he here relates. It is hidden
with great pains, but it is in him. The gloomy Eugene too, is
not without some kindred touch; for, when that appalling
Lady Tippins declares that if Another had survived, he should

have gone down at the head of her list of lovers—and also
when the mature young lady shrugs her epaulettes, and laughs
at some private and confidential comment from the mature
young gentleman—his gloom deepens to that degree that he
trifles quite ferociously with his dessert-knife.   (i, ii, 57)

"Gaffer" Hexam, the "Half savage" boatman, has
been introduced in Chapter One, and his son Charley, "a
curious mixture . . . of uncompleted savagery, and uncompleted civilization," will be introduced in Chapter
Three. It is not too far-fetched to associate with them this
mainly comic savagery of Eugene's in Chapter Two: "his
gloom deepens to that degree that he trifles quite ferociously with his dessert-knife." This mock savagery has
its source in a *depth* of feeling—"his gloom *deepens*"—
which is notable in a chapter of surfaces; we recall that
Gaffer's boat was "Allied to the bottom of the river rather
than the surface," and I have already alluded to Charley's
arrival at the Veneerings' as an eruption from beneath
the surface of society. Eugene's gloominess, too, is related to an instinct for what lies within or behind the surfaces of things. His gloom is like that of the Veneerings'
"melancholy retainer," who is perpetually "gloomy" because he knows the inner constitution of things: "Mean-
time the retainer goes round, like a gloomy Analytical
Chemist: always seeming to say, after 'Chablis, sir?'—
'You wouldn't, if you knew what it was made of.' "
Eugene's and Mortimer's "weakness"—their feeling for
what lies beyond the surface of identities or the recorded
surface of events—is itself hidden, although the narrator,
with his own gifts for irony and double-speaking, is
aware of it and, in Mortimer's case, it may be divined
from the linguistic double-facedness of his storytelling.

On the surface, they belong to "good society," and their faces appear in the glass; but "impressibility" is in them.

What is striking about Eugene's revelatory trifling with a blunt knife, however, is that it is occasioned by Lady Tippins' *approval* of the story and apparent agreement with its moral point. The "appalling Lady Tippins declares that if Another had survived, he should have gone down at the head of her list of lovers." This is the list of lovers that Dickens calls "a grisly little fiction"—Lady Tippins is one of Dickens' grotesques of aging flirtation—and both Mortimer and Eugene appear in it. By her gesture of including Another in the list, Lady Tippins reveals that her response to the story is a trivializing sentimentality, based on a reductive comprehension of its human content. In other words, she responds to the story on precisely that conventional-romance level that Mortimer is savaging, and it is this response that enrages Eugene. The list of lovers, the official Register, the conventional story of poverty and romance: each of these "printed forms" fixes and diminishes the lived life, love, or death in a way that, according to "Society's" perverse convention, it is "civilized" to accept, "savage" to resist.

When Mortimer continues his story, after its emotional climax, he bristles anew with resentment against the conventions of his temporary occupation: "We must now return, as the novelists say, and as we all wish they wouldn't . . ." His impressibility is such, by now, that the burden of the distorting form is literally too much for him. He leaves out the important detail of Old Harmon's death, just as, at the beginning of the story, he forgets where "Somewhere" is, and must be coaxed into coherent narration by one of the Buffers.

To see Mortimer toiling, from beginning to end, under the yoke of narrative form is instructive for the case of his creator. The most important function of his story is to provide a thorough exposition of what precedes the recorded action of the novel Dickens is "telling." But Mortimer trying to tell the story within the assigned convention and also to signal his feeling for a deeper reality than the convention can convey is an image to set beside what I have been calling the parable of the looking-glass, Dickens' indirect discrediting of representational form. The fact that the story is brought to a temporary conclusion by Charley's interruption—that is, by the story Dickens is telling—which brings news just at the moment that it is required by the story's narrative form, suggests that Mortimer the storyteller is a reflected image of Dickens the novelist.[28] The suggestion is supported to some extent by the possible allusion to *Martin Chuzzlewit*. If that is so, it is hardly stretching a point to say that Mortimer's discontent with his necessary and appropriate form may be a distressed apologetic from Dickens, early in the novel, late in the career. He has had no choice but to tell his stories as "the novelists" do, and, in so doing, to distort as they do the deeper truths. All fictions partake of the reductive nature of Lady Tippins' "grisly little fiction." Everyone lives, as Harmon's daughter did, a life whose story, if told, would be falsified by the very act of storytelling, by the imposition of story form. But compassion and, with it, some intuition of the truth may be lodged in the interstices of that form. By sarcasm like Mortimer's, or by other means, like those of Dickens himself or Tolstoy, the narrative artist may signal to us his own awareness of the falsehood he has no choice but to perpetrate if he wishes to tell the truth at all.

The dilemma of these artists is illuminated by a passage that comes early in Georg Lukács' *Theory of the Novel*, though Lukács would have denied its application to Tolstoy. He is describing and deploring the "disintegration" of the modern world as opposed to the wholeness and "totality" of the Greek. In the modern, the world's "inadequacy" ironically becomes

the precondition for the existence of art and its becoming conscious. This exaggeration of the substantiality of art is bound to weigh too heavily upon its forms: they have to produce out of themselves all that was once simply accepted as given; in other words, before their own *a priori* effectiveness can begin to manifest itself, they must create by their own power alone the preconditions for such effectiveness—an object and its environment. A totality that can be simply accepted is no longer given to the forms of art: therefore they must either narrow down and volatilise whatever has to be given form to the point where they can encompass it, or else they must show polemically the impossibility of achieving their necessary object and the inner nullity of their own means. And in this case they carry the fragmentary nature of the world's structure into the world of forms.[29]

Not one or the other, however, but both of the options given by Lukács are taken by Dickens and Tolstoy: They "narrow down" the real until they can "encompass" it within the closure of forms, and so place before us "the object and its environment"; but in so doing they transgress against their own conviction of reality's resistance to form ("the fragmentary nature of the world's structure"); and so, by allegorizing the demolition of their

chosen or inevitable forms, they demonstrate the "impossibility of achieving their necessary object."

What is so useful about Lukács' insight, moreover, is
that it locates the mimetic activity of the modern artist in
the latter option, the demonstrated rejection of form,
rather than in the creating of "the object and its environment." That the purposes of such artists are indeed mimetic is apparent in the very desperation that powers the
self-destruction of their forms. They despair of representing by formal means that reality which is formless by nature, and they imitate instead the form-destroying activity of reality in the real world. But they do not *only*
imitate this activity, or allegorize it by means of such a
figure as Pierre or Charley. As Lukács implies in saying
that they *"carry* the framentary nature of the world's
structure *into* the world of forms," they actually seek to
open their creations to the form-destroying force of reality itself.[30] Unlike the Veneerings or Anna Schérer, they
invite the world to dine, the whole outlying world, actually intending that the house of fiction will be burst.

It is something like this openness that is suggested
in *Our Mutual Friend* by the arrival *ab extra* of the news of
Harmon's drowning precisely at the moment required by
Mortimer's storytelling. There is in this detail a con-
vergence, a contiguity of the real world and the world of
the story's form, that is fulfilling to the latter but does not
betray the independence, "the stubbornness of the actual."[31] As Mortimer's own surprise and that of his lis-
teners tells us, his story did not by its form predetermine
the completion it gets, as the closure of "coherential"
form would require. It is open instead to a completion

from without, and even then the sense of completeness is illusory and premature.

I have noted previously the possible objection to this line of argument, that the attempted demolition of form within a novel becomes itself a formal element, that repeated demolitions succeed only in forming a structure of repetitions, that is, a new form; I have also noted that such an objection is associated with the view of a novel as a world in itself. Critics committed to such a view will likewise reject the distinction implicit in the foregoing paragraphs, between the imitation of reality in a work of art, and the "openness and receptivity" (Lukács) of the latter to the influence and penetration of the real. If, the argument goes, a "reality" is somehow present to us in a novel, as, for example, the Napoleonic invasion is present in *War and Peace*, then we have before us the evidence that it has been assimilated into the novel's artistic form. The classic statement of such a view in the Dickens bibliography is J. Hillis Miller's *Charles Dickens: The World of His Novels*, which treats each of the novels it discusses as "the transformation of the real world of Dickens' experience into an imaginary world with certain special qualities of its own, qualities which reveal in their own irreplaceable way Dickens' vision of things."[32] The "transformation" of the real world into the Dickensian is, like the "assimilation" of matter into form described by Wellek and Warren, thorough and seamless; but Miller usefully complicates the issue by leading us half-way back, as it were, to the real world. The "special qualities" of the Dickens world "reveal" to us not the real world, but the world as Dickens saw it, his "vision of things"—

a world view which was, it is commonly felt, highly idio-
syncratic. The point is, I take it, that we cannot get from
the world of Dickens' novels to the world of our experience, nor is it the purpose of interpretation (or reading)
to do so. Rather we can inspect the Dickens world for its
phenomenal qualities, and derive from these, in a systematic way, the characteristics of the Dickens vision. But
the final thrust of this, it is clear, falls somewhat short of
mimesis. The reader arrives, by way of the world of
Dickens' novels, not at reality, but epistemology.

In taking this view, however, one presupposes a
great deal that we have seen to be problematic. We have
seen, for example, that Dickens questions whether any
organizing epistemology or "vision of things" can be sufficient—sufficiently open or plastic—for the formlessness
and sprawl of reality. As I have said, it is precisely in its
resemblance to Dickens' most characteristic style and
means of representation that the mirror has its subtlest
significance for *Our Mutual Friend*. It is a parable by
Dickens about how reality eludes even the Dickensian
vision of things. And it becomes especially relevant in
this connection to see just why Dickens found it ridicu-
lous and contemptible in Podsnap to let epistemology
dictate aesthetics directly. The first reason, already considered, is that Podsnap's epistemology is itself falsely
limiting and hypocritical. He does not admit things he
knows to be real because they "affront" him. But another
reason, more general in its application, may now be ven-
tured: that, for Dickens, all epistemologies are false epistemologies, by virtue of the mental act of imposing form
upon reality in which they consist. Dickens' own epistemology, if it may be called one, seems indeed to have

been that reality is forever escaping our grasp, forever going deeper than, forever superseding and outdistancing, the forms provided by the chasing mind. The problem with the idea that, in Dickens' novels, the real world is smoothly transformed into an imaginary world of Dickens' own is that it assumes either that Dickens thought the real world susceptible to such transformation, or that he was *content* to offer a "transformed" reality—that is, a version of reality reduced and limited by the necessities of artistic form, or of those forms inherent in his own distinctive vision. We see such a version of reality in the mirror that hangs on the Veneering's "brand-new" dining-room wall, or trace its lineaments in the conventional romance form within which Mortimer strains discontentedly to tell his story. In both cases we are aware of Dickens' claustrophobic unrest.

2. The Hollow Down by the Flare: *Our Mutual Friend* Continued

I scarcely dare to speak about the second novel, on which I have been working for a long time, so complicated are the problems involved and so primitive is the vocabulary which the aesthetic of realism—in its present state—offers me. The formal difficulties are enormous; I have constantly to construct models. Anyone who saw me at work would think I was only interested in questions of form. I make these models because I would like to represent reality.[1]

The writer is Bertolt Brecht, the title of his essay is "Against Georg Lukács," and his subject is the limitations of "the aesthetic of realism—in its present state." Lukács' admiration for Tolstoy and Balzac, according to Brecht, prevents him from recognizing as valid the representational or realist aims of twentieth-century experiments with the novel form, such as, in particular, *Ulysses*. For Lukács, there is form inherent in the real world—not static, but dialectical—and this form the masters of realism grasped and succeeded in revealing to us. Brecht says that he wishes to reveal, instead, that latter-day awareness of what we have already seen Lukács describe as the "fragmentary nature of the world's structure." By no means forsaking the representational aims of realism, Brecht seeks to convey that fragmentation by tampering with models of form.

My own argument so far has taken a direction allied to Brecht's. I have extended his argument backwards into the last century to say, "against Georg Lukács," that classical realists such as Dickens and Tolstoy experiment, like Brecht, with models and formal constructs and paradigms, and for substantially the same reason, that is, in order to represent reality. Like Pierre Bezhúkov, who takes up Bonapartism, freemasonry, philanthropy, numerology and other systems in turn, in search of a program which will account entirely for the seeming chaos of his existence, the realists take up and discard models in search of that which will serve the ideal of open form: a form which can sustain the "fictive object" in an "environment" (Lukács) that is not artificially insulated against reality, that is open, in other words, to a potentially disruptive penetration from without. The fictive object can, of course, be representational in the usual sense, that is, it can imitate, or stand for, some object in the real world. But form, too, according to this ideal, can be representational. It can represent, by its openness, the vulnerability of human design and intention in the real world. And here again the example of Tolstoy's Pierre is relevant. Ultimately he accedes to the philosophy of the peasant Platón Karatáev, which claims to account systematically for nothing at all, and is in fact skeptical of the capacity of consciousness to take in the truth of the world. By this modesty it enables one, in the closing words of the second Epilogue, to "recognize a dependence of which we are not conscious." This paradox—the paradox of consciously recognizing that of which we are not conscious, but upon which we nonetheless depend—is equivalent to the paradox of open form, which attempts to acknowledge fully that which lies beyond itself, and is greater than itself, and inclusive of itself. They are in fact the identical paradox, for one may say of such a consciousness that it is open in form.

The key word in Tolstoy's formula, for his purposes as for ours, is "dependence": a "dependence of which we are not conscious." Pure form, if such a thing were possible, would tend to radical independence, to autonomy; and the will to artistic form is to some extent, surely, an expression of the desire of consciousness to deny its own inevitable contingency, its dependence on the external world for the meaningful reference of its "content." But dependence on the real world is the first fact of realism, and to demonstrate openness to the fact of this dependence is the paradoxical function of form in realist art.

To this ideal of openness we may contrast what Dickens' narrator in *Our Mutual Friend* tells us of the mind and character of Bradley Headstone:

Bradley Headstone, in his decent black coat and waistcoat, and decent white shirt, and decent formal black tie, and decent pantaloons of pepper and salt, with his decent silver watch in his pocket and its decent hairguard round his neck, looked a thoroughly decent young man of six-and-twenty. He was never seen in any other dress, and yet there was a certain stiffness in his manner of wearing this, as if there were a want of adaptation between him and it, recalling some mechanics in their holiday clothes. He had acquired mechanically a great store of teacher's knowledge. He could do mental arithmetic mechanically, sing at sight mechanically, blow various wind instruments mechanically, even play the great church organ mechanically. From his early childhood up, his mind had been a place of mechanical stowage. The arrangement of his wholesale warehouse, so that it might be always ready to meet the demands of retail dealers—history here, geography there, astronomy to the right, political economy to the left—natural history, the physical sciences, figures, music, the lower mathematics, and what not, all in their several places—this care had imparted to his countenance a look of care; while the habit of questioning and being questioned had given him a suspicious manner, or a manner that would be better described as one of lying in wait. There was a kind of settled trouble in the face. It was the face belonging to a naturally slow or inattentive intellect that had toiled hard to get what it had won, and to hold it now that it was gotten. He always seemed to be uneasy lest anything should be missing from his mental warehouse, and taking stock to assure himself.

Suppression of so much to make room for so much, had given him a constrained manner, over and above. Yet there was enough of what was animal, and of what was fiery (though smouldering), still visible in him, to suggest that if young Bradley Headstone, when a pauper lad, had chanced to be told off for the sea, he would not have been the last man in a ship's crew. Regarding that origin of his he was proud, moody, and sullen, desiring it to be forgotten. And few people knew of it.   (II, i, 266–67)

I have already noted that the action of *Our Mutual Friend* rests or depends on a substratum of primary reality: the river, which flows through the book in company with such liquid analogues as mud, blood, and sweat; the ubiquity of dust and ashes, the elemental stubbornness of iron and stone;[2] and, within, a core of instinct, "a word," says the narrator, "we all clearly understand" (II, v, 320), and which was "quite familiar knowledge down in the depths of the slime, ages ago" (III, xiv, 647). No character is more thoroughly a creature of this lurking, primordial dimension of the world than Headstone. But it is plain from the above that his consciousness has been developed into its present state precisely by the act of suppressing, forgetting and denying this dependence, and building a bulwark of systematic information and orderly "knowledge" against it.

Dickens establishes the resulting restlessness of repressed instinct in the man by describing the visible "want of adaptation" between the "fiery," "animal" self and the "decency" of his costume and social role, and this discrepancy is reinforced by the metaphorical figures he uses. Headstone is a machine, mechanical even in the performance of music—and the choice of music as an example of his skills may carry the suggestion, supported elsewhere in the novel, that what instincts are trapped beneath the mechanical surface may be spiritual and beautiful as well as "animal." The figure of machine is changed to that of a warehouse: "From his early childhood up, his mind had been a place of mechanical stowage." It is interesting that as the image develops, Headstone figures as the careworn keeper of the warehouse rather than the warehouse itself, implying a relevant distance between mind and self. The observation which follows, to the effect that Headstone would have made a good sailor, is arguably a metaphorical way of saying that if the schoolmaster had lived in more honest and direct relation to the true sources of his character, and to the primal sources of all life (the sea), an integrated and authentic selfhood would have been possible. "But regarding that origin of his, he was proud, moody, and sullen, desiring it to be forgotten." Along the way, the "want of adaptation" between the conscious and the unconscious self is explicitly figured in terms of the closure and insularity of the former, at least once. His is described as an "intellect that had toiled hard to get what it had won, and that had to hold it now that it was gotten. He always seemed to be uneasy lest anything should be missing from his mental warehouse."

The symptoms of this radical "want of adaptation," which roughly diagnoses, if one wishes to say so, as schizophrenia, Dickens illustrates by endowing his character's behavior with certain gestures of self-destruction, physical expressions of the revolt of the subliminal. These include, eventually, the grinding of his fist into the churchyard wall when he swears revenge on Wrayburn, and the sudden bursting of a blood vessel in his nose near the book's climax. This series of gestures begins with Headstone's first appearance in the novel:

"Look here, Hexam." Mr Bradley Headstone, highly certificated stipendiary schoolmaster, drew his right forefinger through one of the buttonholes of the boy's coat, and looked at it attentively. "I hope your sister may be good company for you?"

"Why do you doubt it, Mr Headstone?"

"I did not say I doubted it."

"No, sir; you didn't say so."

Bradley Headstone looked at his finger again, took it out of the buttonhole and looked at it closer, bit the side of it and looked at it again.

"You see, Hexam, you will be one of us. In good time you are sure to pass a creditable examination and become one of us. Then the question is—"

The boy waited so long for the question, while the

schoolmaster looked at a new side of his finger, and bit it, and looked at it again, that at length the boy repeated:

"The question is, sir—?"

"Whether you had not better leave well alone." (II, i, 265)

Headstone's exterior is designed to display what is respectable and decent, and to disguise the rest; his self-destructive tics, such as biting the side of his finger, are the revenge of the depths against the deceitful surface (compare mirrors). In this exchange with Hexam, we can see that Headstone's linguistic style is deceitful in the same way. He refuses to be direct about his doubts concerning Lizzie, to be frank about his instinct to repress such an element as Lizzie represents in Charley's life. His language, it may be said, has the same repressive structure as his consciousness. And the disruptive promptings from within are the counterpart in one instance of characterization—and indeed a moral and thematic counterpart—to the formal condition I have been describing, the revolt of content against the limits of form.

Headstone, it is generally recognized, is an antagonist of rather unique interest in the Dickens *œuvre*. It is not only that, in the complexity of his make-up, he surpasses, say, Rigaud and Carker, and even, to be fair, Scrooge and Jonas Chuzzlewit. None of these is entirely lacking in psychological complexity or depth. The special interest in Headstone's case, rather, is that the conflicts thus complexly rooted are themselves more familiar and "normal," closer to home. He is that rarest of villains in Dickens, the ordinary man gone wrong for ordinary reasons, if to a degree and with an energy that are beyond the ordinary. What is horrific in Bradley Headstone may be exaggerated in our eyes, as Grahame Smith suggests, by his resemblance to the goose-stepping Europeans of the 1930's. If so, that resemblance is neither accidental nor irrelevant, for Dickens has fixed the social background, dislocation, and aspirations of the upward-mobile schoolteacher in such a way that his situation is in its chief features similar to that of the masses out of which fascism made its rise.[3] That class transitions and dislocations of the sort that Bradley Headstone experienced were capable of producing political or private passions the opposite of wholesome and democratic, scornful of both rich (Eugene) and poor (Lizzie), and characterized by a neurotic need for "order" is a bit of prescience that testifies, if further testimony is needed, to how well and deeply Dickens apprehended the intercourse of psychology and sociology in the social conditions of the world in which he set his novels, his assessments of which, when stated directly, so often seem open to attack as simplistic or naive. In the creation of Headstone Dickens made a statement to us about man and society that was realistic in the usual, and the most profound, sense of the word. He was right, it turned out, about the real world.

Dickens was frequently "realistic" or right in this way. Chesterton remarked that Dickens had the knack of protesting abuses that had not yet come about. To establish what is anomalous about Bradley Headstone as a character, brief reference to Watt's theory of realism is in order. Watt draws a useful distinction between "realism of presentation," with which he primarily identifies the tradition of realism in the genre, and "realism of assessment," a wisdom or insight into the true nature of human affairs which may or may not accompany the "tedious asseveration of literal authenticity."[4] Of course, Dickens often brought the two together—the river in *Our Mutual Friend,* for example, is presented with a wonderful exactness of physical impression, but participates at the same time in a complex and "realistic" symbolic utterance about man's place in the world—but it is true that he rarely brought them together *in a character,* and almost never with such subtle and thorough psychological consistency as here. Although the creator of Quilp, for example, is ostensibly knowing about the nature of evil, the presentation of Quilp is not to be pressed for "literal authenticity," for the latter is obviously of lesser importance than the moral "assessment" he embodies, and his credibility may be compromised for the purposes of expressing that assessment. And Quilp, in this respect, is nearer the Dickensian rule, for villains especially. Headstone is not the only Dickens character whose conception is psychologically realistic, but he is one of the few who display the realism of their conception realistically, as characters, say, in George Eliot's novels do. Because he was seen in that light by Henry James, Headstone earned the young writer's somewhat grudging respect.[5]

I would argue, however, that the admittedly exceptional complexity of Headstone, his "realism of presentation" which James recognized and which can be recognized in all the above ways, in fact derives from that "want of adaptation" between form and content, in particular the tyrannical suppression of content by form, which we have seen to be the chief structural element of his appearance, language, behavior, and indeed of his very consciousness; and, further, that whatever else is anomalous about Headstone, this structural element itself is by no means exceptional in Dickens' creations. It is the object of sympathetic or satirical investigation in most of his most interesting characters, however unrealistic their presentation. What is more, it is repressive form, precisely, that Dickens' novels as works of art seek to avoid. The peculiar and complicated condition of form that results from this avoidance is, I have been saying, a distinguishing feature of the realist novel generally. The point I wish to make here, not unrelated to Watt's distinction between realisms of presentation and assessment, is that this condition of form in Dickens' novels should itself be regarded as a realism of form. My premise is that a certain grasp of the "world's structure" deserves to be so denominated. Whatever allegiance to the senses realist novels have shown in their tradition of "literal authenticity" and veracity of detail, they have also shown, by their troubled use (or abuse) of form, an allegiance to the intellectual perception that reality defies formulation, that artistic form distorts and changes what it contains so as to make questionable the "deeper," more fundamental veracity of works of art. And in Headstone we can see that this perception itself becomes a theme for the novelist, an idea informing characterization, plot, action, language.

In considering the analogy between novels and Tolstoy's social machine, and Dickens' use of the mirror, it was suggested that the artistic inadequacy of the analogous forms for the novel was linked in some way to a moral judgment that the author was making: in Tolstoy by the explicit thrust of satire in the first chapter, and in Dickens by the implication of the mirror's Podsnappery, among other things. In this connection it is relevant that

Headstone is, first of all, a study of evil. More clearly than in the preceding examples, it can be observed that the author places a negative valuation on a consciousness structured by the particular relation of (psychic or aesthetic) form to (psychic or aesthetic) content we have been studying. Once we have labelled this consciousness repressive, Dickens' judgment may seem, like our own, a foregone conclusion. But what may be deduced from this about Dickens' idea of the nature of evil is difficult to say. It is nothing so simple as saying that Dickens values "instinct" over "decency."[6] It is somewhat nearer to the truth to say that, for Dickens, instincts turned back by a rigid, overweening sense of "decency" take a perverted and destructive course. But the ordering and organizing power of the ego, which cannot be distinguished from its power to repress, and of which the will to artistic form is itself an expression, finds its most palpable expression in *Our Mutual Friend* in the benevolent, elaborate plotting of Harmon and the Boffins to "test" Bella, meaning to cure her of her acquisitive instincts—and Dickens, although it has rarely endeared him to readers of the novel, was never more in earnest than in his approval of their plan.

A more useful contrast to Headstone is provided by Lizzie Hexam, the most wholly good character in the book, and one who seems indeed almost bereft of ego. Her goodness, which is identical with her capacity for self-sacrifice, as is usually the case with the Dickens heroine, is in fact only slightly more credible than her gift for refined speech, which Dickens often bestows when he wishes to signify the great spiritual worth of a character.[7] Notwithstanding these objections, Lizzie is an interesting character, in part because of the great interest

of her relationship with her brother. At issue in that relationship is the opposition between the values of dependence and autonomy, upon one side of which, as we
have seen, the influential figure of Bradley Headstone is
rigidly constructed.

When we first see the younger Hexams together (i,
iii), Charley still lives with his father and sister in the
rundown waterside hovel. Lizzie is telling him the story
of their past, present, and future, which she "reads" by
gazing into "the hollow down by the flare" in the fire-
place. After she recalls to him the days of their early
childhood, in which she was "mother and sister both" to
Charley, he asks her to tell the secrets of the future. She
answers, rendering past and future alike in the present
tense, that she will be found "continuing with father and
holding to father" because she is a "stay" to him, and if
she did not remain "faithful . . . he would—in revenge-
like, or in disappointment, or both—go wild and bad."
But Charley she sees as "divided" from them, eventually,
by the course of his learning and advancement in life.
"But I see, too," she adds "[that] it is a great work to
have cut you away from father's life, and to have made a
new and good beginning." Needless to say, she wants no
such advancement for herself: "I feel my want of learning
very much, Charley. But I should feel it much more, if I
didn't know it to be a tie between me and father" (i, iii,
72–73).

Eventually she is proved right, of course, in her prediction that Charley will progressively cut himself off as
he advances. This will culminate when he cuts himself
off even from Headstone, when the latter's reputation has
been darkened (iv, vii). But her benevolent assumption

that such advancement in social status will have proved a
"great work" is more than doubtful. Shortly after the
death of Gaffer, when Lizzie is living with Jenny Wren
and Charley has begun his career as a "pupil-teacher,"
the latter gives evidence, on a visit to his sister, of having
begun that process of rejection of one's origin and suppression of memories which formed the basis of his master's character. He objects particularly to Lizzie's reason
for living with the dolls' dressmaker, which is that Jenny
is the grandchild of a man whose corpse Gaffer Hexam
had robbed, and Lizzie, by living in the house and as-
sisting Jenny, wishes to make "compensation—restitu-
tion—never mind the word, you know my meaning. Father's grave." As we may expect, Charley "does not
respond with any tenderness" to this sentiment. He is
here at his most reminiscent of Pip:

> "Why can't you let bygones be bygones? Why can't you,
> as Mr Headstone said to me this very evening about another
> matter, leave well alone? What we have got to do, is, to turn
> our faces full in our new direction, and keep straight on."
>
> "And never look back? Not even try to make some
> amends?"
>
> "You are such a dreamer," said the boy, with his former
> petulance. "It was all very well when we sat before the
> fire—when we looked into the hollow down by the flare—but
> we are looking into the real world, now."
>
> "Ah, we were looking into the real world then, Charley!"
>
> "I understand what you mean by that, but you are not
> justified in it. I don't want, as I raise myself, to shake you off,
> Liz. I want to carry you up with me . . . Well, then, don't pull
> me back, and hold me down."   (II, i, 278)

The defining characteristic of Lizzie's consciousness is a
radical apprehension of continuity, in time and in human

relationships. The past exerts moral claims on the present, generations have a kind of moral interdependence, and the future may be read in the conditions of the past and present. All of her predictions about herself and Charley, as well as the prediction she later makes about Bella Wilfer, come true (III, ix, 592). Past and future are immanent in the present, as her use of the present tense for memories and fortune-telling alike suggests. Surely it is the validity of this apprehension of time that is one of the things in question in the dispute over whether "the hollow down by the flare" was or was not a representation of "the real world."

At second glance, the sense of that dispute is rather elusive and wants discriminating. Were the pictures Lizzie saw in the fire "real," as she affirms and he denies? The obvious sense of this exchange is that Lizzie reminds Charley that she has predicted he would cut himself off from her, and he denies the plain fact that this has already begun to take place. But only some of the pictures in the fire were predictions: The rest were memories. In saying that these too were the "real world" Lizzie seems to be near to articulating her evident assumption that the past is "real" and has consequences in the present, in the sense that memories such as she "read" in the fire entail responsibilities that one cannot now neglect with impunity. Perhaps it is this seeing of the past in the fire of the present that Charley is dismissing as "dreaming," rather than the fortune-telling. He sees no reason why one cannot keep "straight on."

> "I am not here selfishly, Charley. To please myself, I cannot be too far from that river."
> "Nor could you be too far from it to please me. Let us get

quit of it equally. Why should you linger about it any more
than I? I give it a wide berth."

"I can't get away from it, I think," said Lizzie, passing her
hand across her forehead. "It's no purpose of mine that I live
by it still."

"There you go, Liz! Dreaming again! You lodge yourself
of your own accord [with Jenny] . . . and then you talk as if
you were drawn or driven there. Now, do be more
practical."   (II, i, 278)

Dickens was not everywhere successful in his attribution
of self-sacrifice to his female characters; later in this
novel, Bella will suffer appreciably in vigor and, simply,
in interest when she succumbs to that virtue. But here, I
think, it adds vigor and interest just where they are
needed. " 'I *can't* get away from it, I think,' said Lizzie,
passing her hand across her forehead. 'It's no purpose of
mine that I live by it still.' " We are given reason to
believe that Lizzie would rather not be so self-sacrificing,
that she is aware of being in the grip of a compulsion of
some kind: an awareness we would not credit in Esther
Summerson or Amy Dorrit. Of course, the novel's reader
has a better understanding of the nature of this compulsion than Lizzie does. The river's claim upon her has its
authority in the abiding primordial substratum of the
novel, suggested here by the confluence of "river" and
"fire" and "blood," with which the memory of her father
is associated. The force of the "primal ooze," which was
Gaffer's professional medium and in which he died, is finally irresistible: irresistible not only to Lizzie, because
this is a novel in which the sources of all things and persons it includes assert themselves sooner or later and
must ultimately be honored in their priority; but especially irresistible to her, given her special openness and

awareness. Moreover, her not-quite-conscious awareness of this elemental level of reality informs her "reading" of the pictures in the fire, and it is by virtue of this that they are "the real world" in the deepest sense. It is in contrast to her awareness, finally, that Charley's sense of what is real or "practical" seems most narrow and obtuse. In his refusal to recognize the reality of that which is behind him and that which, as it were, supports him from beneath, Charley Hexam is East London's version of Podsnap.

It can be seen now that Lizzie's goodness answers Headstone's evil in a fuller way than at first appeared. As the evil of the latter was rooted in a consciousness that was closed or repressive in form, a head of stone, Lizzie's capacity for good, the very idea of morality in her, derives from her earnest acknowledgments of the origins of her personal identity, and of all human life.

One aspect at least of Lizzie's "deeper" awareness ought to be pursued here, and that is its half-conscious, half-unconscious or compulsive nature. She meets the terms of Tolstoy's paradoxical exhortation that one "recognize a dependence of which we are not conscious." Indeed her wisdom resembles that of the peasant Platón Karatáev in more ways than one. The implication in both cases seems to be that a fully conscious formulation of such truths as they somehow grasp would *ipso facto* be destructive of those truths: content, once again, reduced or otherwise distorted by form, in this case even the minimal form of ideation. Charley shows contempt for this kind of wisdom by calling it "dreaming" and elsewhere "fancy," and Headstone, of course, supports him in this contempt. But dreams and fancy are terms more apt than

Charley knows, a good deal closer to the process of Lizzie's knowing than deductive logic or systematic intellec-
tion of any kind.

The chapter with which these last pages have been
concerned is entitled "Of an Educational Character," and
is remarkable for the concision with which the above an-
tinomy is offered up. The chapter begins by introducing
us to Headstone and his kind of knowledge and ends
with the visit to Lizzie and Jenny, during which Lizzie's
dreams and fancies are seen to possess considerable "realism of assessment." On the way from their school to
Lizzie's—on the way, that is, from one of these extremes
to the other—Charley and Headstone pass through a
landscape that is strangely emblematic of their own disorder:

> The schools . . . were down in that district of the flat
> country tending to the Thames, where Kent and Surrey meet,
> and where the railways still bestride the market-gardens that
> will soon die under them. The schools were newly built, and
> there were so many like them all over the country, that one
> might have thought the whole place were but one restless
> edifice with the locomotive gift of Aladdin's palace. They were
> in a neighborhood which looked like a toy neighborhood
> taken in blocks out of a box by a child of particularly
> incoherent mind, and set up anyhow; here, one side of a new
> street; there, a large solitary public-house facing nowhere;
> here, another finished street already in ruins; there, a church;
> here, an immense new warehouse; there a dilapidated old
> country villa; then, a medley of black ditch, sparkling cu-
> cumber-frame, rank field, richly cultivated kitchen-garden,
> brick viaduct, arch-spanned canal, and disorder of frowziness
> and fog. As if the child had given the table a kick, and gone to
> sleep.   (II, i, 267–268)

The newness, with which the pupil and teacher are
identified by their class aspirations and by the very fact

of the "ragged schools," is here associated with a radical discontinuity of past and present, which is the opposite of that continuum which Lizzie perceives, and upon which her morality is based. Moreover the triumph of the disordering imposition of order is predicted unequivocally: "The railroads still bestride the market-gardens that will soon die under them." The old will continue to assert itself, however, and having to do so against the repressive structure of the new, rather than a conceivable plastic or open one, will cause warp and perversion of the kind that Headstone exemplifies in a violent way, and little Miss Peecher, the schoolmistress, in a pacific:

> But, even among school-buildings, school-teachers, and school-pupils, all according to pattern and all engendered in the light of the latest Gospel according to Monotony, the older pattern into which so many fortunes have been shaped for good or evil, comes out. It came out in Miss Peecher, the schoolmistress . . .
>
> Small, shining, neat, methodical, and buxom was Miss Peecher; cheery-cheeked and tuneful of voice. A little pincushion, a little housewife, a little book, a little workbox, a little set of tables and weights and measures, and a little woman, all in one. She could write a little essay on any subject, exactly a slate long, beginning at the left-hand top of one side and ending at the right-hand bottom of the other, and the essay should be strictly according to rule. If Mr Bradley Headstone had addressed a written proposal of marriage to her, she would probably have replied in a complete little essay on the theme exactly a slate long, but would certainly have replied yes. For she loved him. (ii, i, 268)

Her exemplum is bittersweet. A good and harmless creature, whose loving instincts have not been "educated" away, she nonetheless suffers from an addiction to rules and forms—"exactly a slate long"—which is perhaps not unallied to her inability to perceive content in the case of Bradley Headstone. "The decent hair-guard that went around his neck and took care of his decent silver watch was an object of envy to her," says Dickens' narrator, naming, with some irony, just those objects upon which he had previously been careful to focus our scorn for the deceit they embody. This relevant choice of items accents Miss Peecher's naive confidence in the outward form of things. The man she loves is genuinely a monster, in spite of, or because of, his correct and "decent" exterior. I may add, without straying too far from context, that the novel's successful love affairs all depend on a mutual recognition that the lover is *not* what he or she appears to be: John and Bella, Eugene and Lizzie, even Sloppy and Jenny Wren.

Miss Peecher's slate-long essays will serve to bring to the surface again the issue with which this essay has been implicitly concerned all along. Their rigid structure, in which form (dis-)orders content, recalls those "printed forms" of which Mortimer complained, the municipal registers of death and the form of the gift-book romance, or Lady Tippins' "grisly little fiction" of a list of lovers. Ultimately they should recall the novel itself, about whose (dis-)ordering imposition of form upon experience the realist, I have been saying, is concerned. It may be that Dickens hopes for a more positive paradigm of his novels in the picture stories that Lizzie "reads" in the flames. Significantly, those stories were half-products of dreaming and fancy, rather than constructed, as it were, on wholly logical premises.

Lizzie's stories have been sufficiently characterized as "open to the fact of dependence," so that we are ready for a new set of terms. They derive from Roman Jakobson: "The primacy of the metaphoric process in the literary schools of romanticism and symbolism has been repeatedly acknowledged, but it is still insufficiently realized that it is the predominance of metonymy which underlies and actually predetermines the so-called "realistic" trend.[8]" In context, Jakobson is concerned with the principle governing selection of figurative language. Governance by the principle of metaphor, that is, would mean the displacement or substitution of one term by another drawn from a context in which the first is not ordinarily found; whereas selection governed by the principle of metonymy would displace terms by others with which they are associated in their familiar environments, for example, the White House for the Presidency. Jakobson's example of the latter is taken from Tolstoy, wherein a woman is represented by an article of her attire; from the present discussion the example of Headstone's hairguard suggests itself.

Jakobson's claim that the metonymic principle of selection predominates in realism is a valuable and accurate description of the linguistic surface typical of texts in that tradition. Because generally we follow Watt on the presentation of detail as the primary criterion for realism, most of us would endorse Jakobson fully. I do not hesitate to do so, although the proportions of metonymy and metaphor in many Dickensian figures is extremely problematic. The language of *Moll Flanders* is one long piece of metonymy, mostly undiverted by metaphor. Dickens does not write realist novels in that most obvious sense in which *Moll Flanders* is one. At this point I want only to adopt the metonymy-metaphor distinction, and the association of metonymy and realism, as a description of possible attitudes toward the novel form, in respect of which, it may be, Dickens does indeed write realist novels.

It will be clear at once, I think, what is meant by metaphoric versus metonymic form in a novel. A novel which is metaphoric in form constitutes a discrete, homogeneous "world in itself, of illusions and symbolic forms" (Wellek) which substitutes for the real world, for analogical purposes. It is a model of the real world, with significant similarities and differences.[9] A novel metonymic in form is less a term substituted for the world than the marking off, with imperfect closure, of a certain area of experience actually located on the world's horizon. In his aspiration to "open" or metonymic form, the realist intends that our experience of his novel will converge horizontally, as it were, with our experience of life.

Until this point I have concerned myself with the theoretical underpinnings and consequences of metonymic form. As a result, perhaps, more has been said about the ideal form of realist novels than about the form of the text at hand. And yet it is possible to suggest here a strategy for the interpretation of *Our Mutual Friend* along the lines of the theoretical argument heretofore developing.

Our Mutual Friend is full of "cunning artificers" (I, vii, 122). The novel is moved along by plotting, conspiracy, and connivance, by the Lammles, Fledgeby, Riderhood, and Wegg; by pretenders, variously motivated dissimulators, such as Harmon and Boffin and Mrs. Wilfer; characters who devise a more or less permanent mask, of irony or of "decency," such as Lightwood and Wrayburn, or Headstone and the "Honest Labourer" Riderhood. We may first inquire into the causes and intentionality behind the artifice, and the moral-thematic issues to which these are related. But then the artifact itself—the money-getting scheme, the mask or persona, or such elaborate performances as Boffin the miser, or Mortimer or Lizzie as storytellers—may be inspected for formal qualities *qua* artifact. As with Headstone and Lizzie Hexam, the question of how "open" a construction obtains in the individual case will be seen to have a direct relation to the characterization of the artificer, to his symbolic role, his plot-function, and so on. Finally the artifact may be inspected for its analogical implications for the artifact of Dickens' making, the novel as a whole.

2

It is mildly paradoxical that Jenny Wren and Mr Venus should rank, as they do, among Dickens' most outlandish, least realistic inspirations.[10] In the ordinary sense of the word, they are the only two "artificers" in *Our Mutual Friend,* and their crafts are paradigms of mimetic or representational art. In the novelist's presentation of their crafts, moreover, there is a striking similarity, which now calls for attention. It is that we are no sooner familiar with their skill and competence as artisans, than we are made aware of certain mimetic deficiencies or limitations in the art they practice—in other words, of what it is these artists cannot imitate.

There is every reason to believe, at first, Mr. Venus' boast that he is a "workman without an equal" in his chosen field: "Mr. Wegg, if you was brought here loose

in a bag to be articulated I'd name your smallest bones
blindfold equally with your largest, as fast as I could pick
'em out, and I'd sort 'em all, and sort your wertebrae, in
a manner that would equally surprise and charm you'' (I,
vii, 128). His successful works seem to justify his pride.
''There's animation!'' he says of a preserved canary. ''On
a twig, making up his mind to hop!'' (I, vii, 125). Nevertheless, in our first view of him, we find Mr. Venus pro-
fessionally stumped. His difficulty proceeds from the fact
that skeletons to be articulated do not always arrive with
their complete numbers of bones. Such skeletons must be
completed with bones from a miscellaneous bin, denominated ''human warious.'' Now the bone from Silas
Wegg's lost leg has ended up in such a lot, and Wegg discovers, when he comes to bargain for the return of it, that
Venus has had, inexplicably, no success in working the
leg into a ''miscellaneously'' assembled skeleton:

   ''And how have I been going on, this long time,
Mr. Venus?''
   ''Very bad,'' says Mr. Venus, uncompromisingly.
   ''What? Am I still at home?'' asks Wegg, with an air of
surprise.
   ''Always at home.''
   This would seem to be secretly agreeable to Wegg, but he
veils his feelings, and observes, ''Strange. To what do you
attribute it?''
   ''I don't know,'' replies Venus, who is a haggard,
melancholy man, speaking in a weak voice of querulous
complaint, ''to what to attribute it, Mr. Wegg. I can't work you
into a miscellaneous one, no how. Do what I will, you can't be
got to fit. Anybody with a passable knowledge would pick you
out at a look, and say,—'No go! Don't match!' ''
   ''Well, but hang it, Mr. Venus,'' Wegg expostulates with

some little irritation, "that can't be personal and peculiar in
me. It must often happen with miscellaneous ones."

"With ribs (I grant you) always. But not else." (I, vii, 124)

Where Wegg refers to his lost leg as himself ("And how
have I been going on, this long time, Mr. Venus?"), a
curious effect obtains, whose name, of course, is synecdoche: a substitution of a part for the whole. But Venus'
bafflement, in light of his anatomical expertise, seems in
a way to validate the synecdochic substitution. At least in
this instance, that is, the parts of men are not transfer-
able, and one way of explaining this is to say that each
part is imbued, however invisibly to expert scrutiny,
with some trace of the essence of the original whole,
preventing its assimilation into other, alien wholes.
Wegg's leg is exceptional in this respect, but intran-
sigence is the rule, it turns out, in the matter of ribs.
"When I prepare a miscellaneous one," Mr. Venus goes
on, "I know beforehand that I can't keep to nature, and
be miscellaneous with ribs, because every man has his
own ribs, and no other man's will go with them" (I, vii,
124). That is, one may reassemble the original pieces according to rule, but substitutions will violate the representational standard to which Venus explicitly owes allegiance: truth to nature, as nature is known to
anatomical science.

His inability to place Wegg's leg is not the only frustration Venus suffers. The other is rather amatory than
professional, but it is not unrelated to business:

"Mr. Wegg, I'm thirty-two, and a bachelor. Mr. Wegg, I love
her. Mr. Wegg, she is worthy of being loved by a Potentate!"
Here Silas is rather alarmed by Mr. Venus' springing to his

feet in the hurry of his spirits, and haggardly confronting him
with his hand on his coat collar; but Mr. Venus, begging
pardon, sits down again, saying, with the calmness of despair,
"She objects to the business."

"Does she know the profits of it?"

"She knows the profits of it, but she don't appreciate the
art of it, and she objects to it. 'I do not wish,' she writes in
her own hand-writing, 'to regard myself, nor yet to be
regarded, in that boney light.' "   (I, vii, 128)

There is irony already in the notion of a man named
Venus who traffics in carcasses and skeletons, irony
which is compounded by his failure in love. The province of love is, Pleasant Riderhood seems to know, the
province of soul, of essence, that element of the human
composition which Mr. Venus' "boney," meaning skele-
tal or structural, representations do not in fact represent.
She seems to say in her own way that the presumption of
soul necessary to love (of herself by herself or by Venus:
"to regard myself nor yet to be regarded") cannot be
maintained in the "boney light" of Venus' profession,
that is, the anatomical-structural view of man, which sees
him as a whole no greater than an ordered structure of
parts.

Pleasant's remarkable phrase casts a retrospective
light of its own on the scene in Mr. Venus' dismal shop.
Venus' frustration over Wegg's bone can be seen to proceed from a misapprehension attributable to the same
"boney light." Venus sees no reason from a "boney"
viewpoint why the leg resists assimilation, because he
reckons, *qua* anatomist, without that "essence" by which
part belongs to whole. And his boast about the stuffed
canary—"There's animation!"—stands exposed as a sig-

nificant infelicity of expression. It is precisely "animation" in the proper sense that is lacking in the ex-bird.

Now I would stress here that the canary's structure, inside and out, is that of a live canary, and that its imitation of an attitude from life is likewise exact: "On a twig, making up its mind to hop!" He is one of what Mr. Venus calls the "lovely trophies of my art." But in the "boney light" of that art, as indeed literally in the dark shop, there is no basis for distinguishing a live bird from a dead one. One may be taken for the other, because the distinction is other than "boney." The rather crucial difference between the bird in its original state and its representation by art, in other words, is signally overlooked. This overlooking of the definitive essence of life, which renders Venus' art fatal to romance, is also, it can thus be said, a mimetic failure. Moreover, this capacity to confound the living and the dead is, in the context of the novel, instinct with suggestion of another kind. The novel turns, after all, on the mistaking of a live man (Harmon) for a dead one.

Jenny Wren, the dolls' dressmaker, is quite as skilled an artisan as Venus. Like Venus, she copies exactly from life. Not only is the design of dress copied, but, just as Venus' canary strikes a "lifelike" pose, the dolls are outfitted for imitations of real activities, such as weddings, funerals, and presentations at court. What it is that Jenny is unable to imitate she describes to Eugene Wrayburn in a speech that is as touching as it is unnerving and bizarre:

"For when I was a little child," [she says] in a tone as though it were ages ago, "the children that I used to see early in the

morning were very different from any others that I ever saw.
They were not like me; they were not chilled, anxious, ragged,
or beaten; they were never in pain. They were not like the
children of the neighbours; they never made me tremble all
over, by setting up shrill noises, and they never mocked me.
Such numbers of them too! All in white dresses, and with
something shining on the borders, and on their heads, that I
have never been able to imitate with my work, though I know
it so well. They used to come down in long bright slanting
rows, and say all together, 'Who is this in pain! Who is this in
pain!' When I told them who it was, they answered, 'Come
and play with us!' When I said, 'I never play! I can't play!'
they swept about me and took me up, and made me light.''
(ii, ii, 290)

Jenny can imitate the white dresses, but not the shining
"something" on the borders of the dress and about their
heads. The ethereal visitors are, of course, dead children,
angels. Later, from the paradisical retreat on the roof of
Pubsey & Co., Jenny will echo their soothing exhortation
to the living, "Come up and be dead!" (ii, v, 335). Thus
what Jenny cannot imitate in her work is in one sense the
opposite of that spark of life which evaded Venus' re-crea-
tions. But the art of both is restricted and disabled in the
same way. They are bound by a mimetic convention of
literal veracity, of exact replication of what the eye sees,
in accordance with empirical knowledge, a convention
that prevents them from representing what seems to
them most essential in reality. Venus and Jenny are like
each other, significantly, in placing the highest possible
valuation on just the elements which elude their respective works. However loveless the "lovely trophies" of
Venus' art, Venus' love is in fact his defining obsession,
as his name suggests, just as Jenny's visions, of children

as of birds and flowers, are meant, surely, to bear the deepest witness to her true nature. But in spite of this, and in spite of their skills, neither can produce anything more than literal replicas, unimproved by either the warm inspiration of life or the transcendent spirituality of the angelic dead.

This way of putting the matter will recall the dilemma of Mortimer as storyteller. He could be accurate as to the facts of the story, but felt, throughout, that something was missing, *necessarily,* from the narration as a whole. In that case, the missing "something" could be described as a sense of the actuality of the human suffering involved in the events of the story, actuality which the story form itself diminished. Now my purpose in examining the arts of Jenny Wren and Mr. Venus has not been merely to add two more to the list of mimetic paradigms in *Our Mutual Friend,* but rather to add two examples whose peculiarities will help define further that element of reality which, according to each of the paradigms in their different ways, is characteristically excluded by mimetic form. Until now, it has been sufficient to say that what eluded the necessary form of novels was formlessness *per se.* So much granted, it has been possible to argue that what characterizes realist novels is not so much the verisimilitude or mimetic exactness of their contents, but something teleological instead: their desire to suggest incrementally, to "confess," as it were, the actuality of the outlying, formless real world. Nor is this teleological definition an invitation to vague speculation about the intentions of novelists. The teleology has specific, recognizable consequences for the form of realist novels. The animating spark which eludes Venus' creations and the spiritualizing halo which Jenny cannot copy, and without which her works are inert imitations, suggest still more about the reality that form excludes. They suggest that what is excluded has, if recognized or "confessed" by form, the power to actualize, to vitalize, to "animate" what is contained; and, conversely, that where the exclusion of form is not confessed, what is contained is dead, inert, unreal, whatever its degree of verisimilitude. This is so because the excluded is precisely the locus of the larger, essential or primary reality on which the contents are dependent for their own reality; as, for example, the world of the Veneerings is dependent on the world of the Hexams, which it excludes. It is recognition of this dependence, rather than verisimilitude, that constitutes the realism of the artistic whole.

Common sense must assert itself here, to the effect that if verisimilitude of detail is not constitutive of the enterprise of realism, it is surely not altogether irrelevant to it. What, then, is the relation of verisimilitude to the form of realist novels? One answer is described by Martin Price in his essay on "The Irrelevant Detail and the Emergence of Form." Price is discussing E. H. Gombrich's theory of representation, the central analogy of which, a hobby horse,

can show us that the elaborate forms of realism are generated less by the desire to represent the actual than by the pressure of conventions reaching outward for more complex differentiation. George Eliot, in the famous seventeenth chapter of *Adam Bede*, renounces the easy fictions of romance for the more difficult truths of realism. By this she means an extension of the conventions of romance into a realm where

plots are bent to absorb the actualities of historic life, where
the traditional characters are bleached and thickened until they
become our colorless and undistinguished neighbors. George
Eliot is not offering to give us a literal picture of social reality
but to "give a faithful account of men and things as they have
mirrored themselves in my mind." This is fact becomes an
extension of high forms to include the subliterary, even the
antiliterary, details of a "monotonous homely existence." The
"exact likeness" is the limiting point of the entire process . . .
She sacrifices proportion and the "divine beauty of form" so
as to extend art, as the Dutch painters had, to "those rounded
backs and stupid weatherbeaten faces that have bent over the
spade and done the rough work of the world." The point I
would stress is the deliberate—even militant—extension of
forms rather than the effort at literal representation or record.[11]

Price's concluding "stress" of extension of form over representation, in which I concur, should not obscure the
relationship of necessity that obtains in Eliot's essay. For
Eliot, it is the "faithful representing of commonplace
things"[12] that requires the extending of literary forms.
"High forms" are, as it were, lowered and widened by
the particularizing accretion of realistic detail.

In Dickens, however, there is considerably more to
explain. Forms are, indeed, extended by the accumulation of detail, but what if the details are bizarre, unreal—
the reverse of Eliot's "commonplace"? We may accept as
realistic the teleological extension of forms in a Dickens
novel—in other words, we may recognize that it extends
form *in order to* represent reality—but we may dismiss its
purported realism on other grounds; namely, that the reality it presents is exaggerated or fantastical, at least in
places.

One has not, in the present instance, far to seek for a
suggestion of Dickens' vulnerability on this point. The

"something" clinging to the dress of Jenny's visitors, which she cannot imitate though she "know[s] it so well," is a something the rest of us will be inclined to regard as nothing at all. As it happens, our assessment of Jenny's art is not at issue. In fact she does not even attempt to capture the elusive spirituality she has seen. But it may be that Dickens arrogates this higher mimetic task to his own art. And Jenny herself, considered as a creation and not as a creator, may give evidence of her creator's aspirations of that sort:

> The boy knocked at a door, and the door promptly opened with a spring and a click. A parlour door within a small entry stood open, and disclosed a child—a dwarf—a girl—a something—sitting on a little low old-fashioned arm-chair, which had a kind of little working bench before it.
> "I can't get up," said the child, "because my back's bad and my legs are queer. But I'm the person of the house."
> (II, i, 271)

Jenny is an astounding creature, and the boy, Charley, is astounded. It is the number and variety of unusual traits concentrated in her—none of them quite impossible—which is really so striking: her "sharpness," her reversed relationship to her father, her esoteric daydreams, her endless games with words and names. Abbey Potterson, who has presumably seen a great deal of life, is herself astonished when she receives a visit from Jenny in company with Riah.

As [Riah] stood there, . . . and the little dolls' dressmaker sitting in her golden bower before the fire, Miss Abbey had her doubts whether she had not dreamed those two rare figures . . . and might not wake with a nod next moment and find them gone.

Miss Abbey had twice made the experiment of shutting
her eyes and opening them again, still finding the figures
there . . .   (III, ii, 499–500)

Not incidentally, one way of establishing that a norma-
tive, ordinary reality of setting is at least presumed in a
Dickens novel is to call attention to such scenes as these,
in which more extreme products of Dickens' imagination
appear extreme to characters within the novel. Jenny is
an imitation of nothing that is familiar, either in our
world or in the world of *Our Mutual Friend.* Dickens has
conceived her in some divagation of his mind from the
world he knew, and the world we know.

But the point has already been made that the world
as any of us know it is a world reduced and simplified
and violated by the forms of knowing. Thus we may ask
of any particular divagation from such knowledge if it is
a divagation towards or away from the world as it really
is, out there, beyond our epistemological limits. Consider, along with Jenny's strangeness, the claim that is
made for her "perception" near the end of the book, in
the chapter entitled "The Dolls' Dressmaker Discovers a
Word." She is watching at the bedside of the dying
Eugene (who does not, of course, die):

The dolls' dressmaker, all softened compassion now,
watched with an earnestness that never relaxed. . . . It was
amazing through how many hours at a time she would remain
beside him, in a crouching attitude, attentive to his slightest
moan. As he could not move a hand, he could make no sign of
distress; but, through this close watching (if through no secret
sympathy or power) the little creature attained an
understanding of him that Lightwood did not possess.
Mortimer would often turn to her, as if she were an interpreter
between this sentient world and the insensible man; and she

would change the dressing of a wound, or ease a ligature, or
turn his face, or alter the pressure of the bedclothes on him,
with an absolute certainty of doing right. The natural lightness
and delicacy of touch which had become very refined by
practice in her miniature work, no doubt was involved in this;
but her perception was at least as fine.   (IV, x, 809)

Jenny interprets the "insensible" to the "sentient,"
makes known the unknowable. It is unmistakable that
Jenny's fitness for this mediation has been carefully prepared. It combines her visionary experience with her
craft. Her work had trained her in attentiveness to the
smallest detail, and in lightness of touch. Her word
games are given further meaning when she discovers,
subsequently, the word Eugene is saying (Lizzie's name),
and even her mothering of her father is turned to account
in her nursing of Eugene. Here, in short, all of her oddi-
ties ally themselves as assets with her transcendent "sympathy." By virtue of her sympathy, we are meant to see,
she is in touch with that essence of reality often experienced in Dickens' novels by the dead or dying. She appears on the surface of reality, where her aspect is bizarre, but she belongs, really, to its invisible depths.
She invades, like Charley or Pierre, an ordering conception of the real, Abbey Potterson's (or the novel's) as well
as our own. But she comes from, and represents, a reality
greater and deeper than that we can know: That is, to put
it simply, what Dickens means by her.

    Most objections to Dickens' scenes of death or conva-
lescence address that mordant indulgence of pathetic
emotion which sometimes undeniably attends them,
e.g., the scene of Johnny's death in *Our Mutual Friend* (II,
ix). But at least as distant from modern taste and,

especially, from modern belief is the surfacing, or the superimposition, of this "essential" level of reality that Dickens seems, at such times, to have believed was hovering somewhere above or below the daylight world of the living. Two chapters hence, I will take up *Oliver Twist,* a novel perhaps uniquely suited to serve as the locus of an inquiry into the consequences of this belief for the realism of Dickens' novels. In *Our Mutual Friend,* the importance of two factors may be urged against the deactualizing effect of what appears to be easy or sentimental spirituality.

First, the "essential" dimension of reality that Jenny comes finally to represent is really coextant with the primordial, elemental dimension—of mud, river, decay, blood, sweat, stone—which has been shown to underlie the reality of the novel in a way that is plainly less fantastic. Jenny is said to achieve her mediation of the sentient and the insensible "through this close watching (if through no secret sympathy or power)." The casualness of the parenthesis may be taken to mean that no great distance separates empirical observation (of an intense and superior order, to be sure) from overtly magical or transcendental powers. Such empirical "watching" seems to bring Jenny close to the secret, elemental life of things, and thus to their "essence."

Secondly, it is important to recollect just how the essential-elemental level of reality presents itself in *Our Mutual Friend:* randomly, sporadically, so that it is most easily identified above as a list—mud, blood, and so on. It is compiled, that is, or accumulated, like a dust heap. The novel itself is so compiled, as its wondrous proliferation of "worlds" testifies: six separate spheres of action

are introduced in the first seven chapters. In all of this, as
in paradigms of artistic forms such as the Veneerings'
mirror, it is the unknowability of the real world, its in-
transigence to form, that Dickens stresses. Paradoxically,
it is in his attribution of unreality to any presumptive
formulation of the real that Dickens' strongest claims to
realism subsist.

3. Words and Freedom: Dombey, Clennam, Nell

An affirmation of the real world, an affirmation that realizes itself in the structure and meaning of fiction, is at the heart of the realist's aesthetic. The affirmation survives in our impression of his work even when the realist places before us life's basest realities, for even then he honors life's pre-eminent claims to our attention, sympathy, and concern.

What is other than platitudinous in the above is well suggested by a remark in Kafka's notebooks: "In the war between yourself and the world, back the world." We may be surprised by the authorship of this sunny epigram until we detect the reassuringly Kafkan irony within it: To back the world, you must take sides against yourself. And this negativity toward the self is surely a feature of the aesthetic I am describing. The realist puts in doubt the very enterprise of art. As a corollary of the affirmation of the real, realism discredits the precondition of its own existence, that form which confines, distorts, de-actualizes reality in the process of assimilating it. Indeed, the affirmation begins precisely at the point where reality escapes the clutch of art. And of course the chief thing to be said about the condition of form innocent of crimes against the real—"open" or metonymic form—is that it is ideal and impossible.

The extremity of this formulation may be out of the ordinary, but it accords well enough, no doubt, with the generally conceded notion that what may be called the high aesthetic sensibility is challenged in its premises by the realist tradition developing since Cervantes. The *Quixote* is prototypically that text about which it may be said that it structures itself against its own art because it values reality over artistic renderings of reality, even its own.[1] This self-diminution—it is more explicit than modesty—is at the core of the nineteenth-century realist inheritance from Cervantes through Fielding. George Eliot's lengthy aside to the reader of *Adam Bede*, instanced in the last chapter, only makes plainer what it would have been impossible to deny about her art in any case. Beneath the surface of her writing at most times, an "anti-aesthetic" pressure steadily exerts itself, and it extends to all that is meant by "aesthetic" later in the century and in our own time. Although one would not hesitate to speak of the beauty of her achievement, her gesture of realism is often a gesture of ugliness, whereby the novelist, lacking in general Cervantes' comic resources as an alternative, wilfully disfigures the novel she is writing. Indeed, for a female character in an Eliot novel it can often be a dangerous thing simply to have a pretty face. Late in life, the central modern realist by all counts, Tolstoy, made himself infamous by the quality of attention he gave to the question of the value of art. His most notable fiction, it is true, was behind him when he ranked Harriet Beecher Stowe over Shakespeare on obvious, if stubbornly arguable, grounds. But we have already seen that he intentionally destroyed the potential for grace and symmetry, the pleasing aesthetic wholeness of one of his masterpieces by his manner of paying homage to what he regarded as the irrefragable locus of values, the real historical world.

However, even when the negativity of the realist aesthetic toward nominally artistic values has been conceded, we are likely to demur at its application to Dickens. An art's negation of itself seems, justifiably, the most un-Dickensian of propositions. Everywhere there is evidence that Dickens loves his art, that he exploits with delight the means that his genius has lavished upon him. As is often remarked, Dickens is nearly always at his peak, and nothing is more characteristic of his powers at the peak of their exercise than that they seem to display themselves and celebrate themselves along with or before whatever else they do: describe, entertain, mimic, create. If, in fact, we stress the intransitive sense of the verb "to write," as Roland Barthes has shown good reasons for doing, we may wish to say that what obtains in the Dickens *œuvre* is precisely celebration *rather than* creation.[2] Certainly a quality of stylistic indulgence, self-pleasuring and self-celebrating, with a certain coefficient of joy, attends and conditions the presentation of even the darker scenes in the novels, and inevitably is a part of, and modifies, their dark significances. The scene of Paul Dombey's christening, during the period of mourning for his mother, is not comedy, but satire of the grimmest

sort. Yet Mr. Chick cannot refrain from whistling, and
neither can Dickens:

It happened to be an iron-grey autumnal day, with a shrewd
east wind blowing—a day in keeping with the proceedings.
Mr. Dombey represented in himself the wind, the shade, and
the autumn of the christening. He stood in his library to
receive the company, as hard and cold as the weather; and
when he looked out through the glass room, at the trees in the
little garden, their brown and yellow leaves came fluttering
down, as if he blighted them.

   Ugh! They were black, cold rooms; and seemed to be in
mourning, like the inmates of the house. The books precisely
matched as to size, and drawn up in line, like soldiers, looked
in their cold, hard, slippery uniforms, as if they had but one
idea among them, and that was a freezer. The bookcase,
glazed and locked, repudiated all familiarities. Mr. Pitt, in
bronze, on the top, with no trace of his celestial origin about
him, guarded the unattainable treasure like an enchanted
Moor. A dusty urn at each high corner, dug up from an
ancient tomb, preached desolation and decay, as from two
pulpits; and the chimney-glass, reflecting Mr. Dombey and his
portrait at one blow, seemed fraught with melancholy
meditations.

   The stiff and stark fire-irons appeared to claim a nearer
relationship than anything else there to Mr. Dombey, with his
buttoned coat, his white cravat, his heavy gold watchchain,
and his creaking boots.   (v, 54)

Like the chimney-glass it mentions, the passage reflects
"Mr. Dombey and his portrait at one blow." It is a portrait by metonymy. The things by which he is surrounded reflect attributes of his own "iron-grey autumnal" state of being, a point which is made for us by the
alleged "relationship" of the fire-irons to their owner.[3]
Whatever else we shall wish to say about the passage, we

can be assured, I think, of the thoroughgoing representational accomplishment, the referential utility of every
detail. The inclusion of Pitt and the pulpit-like urns, for
example, are remarkable not only for their aptness in
realistically furnishing the room, but also for extending
the metonymic reach of the description. That is, Pitt and
the pulpits of "desolation and decay" neatly adduce the
political, historical, and religious context of Mr. Dombey's middle-class prosperity.

The portraiture is not, of course, neutral. The narrator discloses his prejudice by remarking of Pitt that he
appears with "no trace of his celestial origin about him,"
an ironic reference to Canning's praise of the Prime Min-
ister as "Heavenborn."[4] The droll tenor of this irony is
familiar. The narrator pretends naiveté, as if he looked
for evidence of celestial origin on Canning's advice, and
expected to find it, so that its absence strikes him as
noteworthy. The absence of celestiality puts in question,
by proximity, Dombey's proud setting up of himself,
which throughout the novel is given a religious me-
taphorization, here reinforced by the religious occasion
of the day. Thus the use of Pitt's bust has a richly con-
ceived representational purpose, and specifically a satirical or deflating one.

But the satirical tone of the interesting little joke is
not really the tone of the passage as a whole. What of the
exclamation "Ugh!"? There the narrator pretends no dis-
appointed sympathy with his subject, but rather exclaims
in open revulsion from it, and, we may want to add,
exclaims with a striking lack of decorum that puts him at
a distance from the decorous scene he describes. It is not,
however, a satirical distance. "Ugh!" is not satire. In the

satirically dissenting opinion on Pitt, the narrator pretends to range himself among Pitt, Canning, and Dombey, while preserving a subtle inner distance of irony.
Here the separation is open and absolute. Small word
that it is, "Ugh!" should alert us to the fact that the narrator's language is not confined by its representational
uses. It is not, like the chimney-glass, only a reflection of
the scene, nor only a satiric refraction of it. It also has, as
it were, a life of its own. It can express reactions independent of either purpose, and can and does assert a
wider independence as well. Thus the chimney-glass is
"fraught with melancholy meditations," while the prose
is strangely playful, though both reflect that same Dombeyism which Dickens takes, of course, so seriously and
finds to be far worse than merely "melancholy" as a subject for meditation.

Playfulness is in evidence in the odd explicitness of
the elaboration of metaphor in the first paragraph. We
are told that "Mr. Dombey represented in himself the
wind, the shade, and the autumn of the christening."
Then his representation of each of these is filled in, ex-
ampled for us as if in game-like fulfillment of the syntac-
tic form: "He stood in his library to receive the company,
as hard and cold as the weather"—wind and shade—
"and when he looked out through the glass room, at the
trees in the little garden, their brown and yellow leaves
came fluttering down, as if he blighted them"—like autumn. What is described here surely furthers the portrait
of Dombey and of the scene, but just as surely the language goes beyond such purposiveness to where it
enjoys the shape of its own expression, the hypothesis-
demonstration form of the trope. The language goes

beyond its usage, that is, to where it affirms itself, we may say, by openly exploiting its own devices.

There is some hint of the willed independence of the language in the description of the books in Dombey's library: "The books precisely matched as to size, and drawn up in line, like soldiers, locked in their cold, hard, slippery uniforms, as if they had but one idea among them, and that was a freezer. The bookcase, glazed and locked, repudiated all familiarities." Dombey's bookshelves recall, perhaps, the library at Gad's Hill, with its false spines of books bearing facetious titles that Dickens himself made up. Dickens' amusement and indignation on this matter are, however, nearly related, and both the description of Dombey's library and Dickens' visual gag in his own library protest against the too rigorous prosecution of the inward or outward form of books. In the passage cited above, the reiteration is somewhat obsessive. The same complaints are repeated without discernible gain: "cold"/"freezer"/"glazed"/"slippery"; "precisely matched"/"drawn up in line, like soldiers"; "hard"/ "locked"/"repudiated all familiarities." The outburst has numerous significances, but in the present case it may be taken primarily to underwrite the liberties the surrounding language is taking, the freedom it is exercising beyond the strict regimen of duty imposed upon the contents of books by a quasi-military conception of form.

The peculiarity of this matter is that it can hardly be stated without being pressed too far. But it is well to see that celebration and affirmation are present in the tone even of Dickens' soberest satire. How solid an objection they pose to any too unsmiling a reading of Dickens may be seen in a backwards glance at the movement of "gloomy" Dickens critics inspired by Edmund Wilson's essay in 1940, "Dickens: The Two Scrooges." Wilson's followers, who included, among others, Edgar Johnson and Graham Greene, sought to found the case for Dickens on his pessimism, his obsession with evil, identification with criminals and murderers—in short, on that darker muse undetected by Chesterton.[5] In a frontal attack on the fortress of Chesterton's Boz, Wilson wrote that even the laughter of Dickens' early comedy "is an exhilaration which already shows traces of the hysterical. It leaps free of the prison of life; but gloom and soreness must always drag it back."[6] Here Wilson's phrase, "the prison of life," is chiefly remarkable: a brief metaphor that begs the entire question of Dickens' world view. But such polemics were very much to the point a generation or two ago. Not only did they render Dickens palatable to the post-war intellectuals who read *La Nausée* with a sense of epiphany; they also promoted the plain truth that the novels were serious, adult. They showed that a wider range and a greater depth of psychological interest subsisted in them than had been recognized at least since Gissing. Indeed, if there were such a thing as a level of paraphraseable meaning in a literary work—a hypothesis which critics unfriendly to Wilson later put in doubt—it was probably right to say that the meaning of (the usual example) *Little Dorrit* is not "optimistic" but "pessimistic," although it should be added that there has never been an intelligent argument for Dickens as nihilist. More complex versions of the meaning of meaning, however, urged the importance of linguistic detail, of unparaphraseable resonance, of tone. On this prompting, readings of Dickens must take into account what Wil-

son's essay does not, the nearly constant effect of celebration, differing of course from comedy, that is never absent for long, and is present even in the Marshalsea.

The point of this avowal in the present context will
not be missed. I have described Dickens' "negative paradigms" of representation and read Mortimer's narration
as an apologetic from his creator for the art of the novel.
Against the negative drift of these instances stands what
is at least as apparent, the artist's energetic indulgence
and endorsement of his creative powers. Perhaps it is not
correct to say that it is his art as a whole that is being en-
dorsed or celebrated by this indulgence, however. The
self-celebration noted in *Dombey* was, precisely, linguistic. It is Dickens' language that is in a condition of celebration: that is to say, his language rather than, in some
wider sense, his art.

The distinction must be paradoxical, of course. His
art, we should not need to be reminded, is made of language. Possibly the intractability of the paradox can be
evaded if one limits radically what is meant by "Dickens'
language," to mean by it something like what is conveyed by the phrase "Dickensian language"—in other
words, his characteristic rhetorical repertoire, tricks he
frequently plays with words, for example, comic
periphrasis. In this sense his "language" may be distinguished from his art as part from whole, for it is in this
sense that we speak of his language as of his plot or his
imagination—perfectly lucid conceptual differentiations,
although the "art" is unified. But there is point in court-
ing the full force of paradox in the distinction between
the language of Dickens and his art.

Having mentioned Roland Barthes, I have already

alluded to a point of view from which the distinction is likely to meet resistance. The stress on the intransitivity of the verb "to write," on the self-referentiality of all language, including or especially literary language, and the impulse to regard what is described or created by language as an illusion to be exposed or "demystified," are products of the confluence of modern linguistics and structural anthropology as it has made itself felt in the field of literary criticism. This confluence is of the greatest relevance to Dickens, as has already begun to be demonstrated, most prominently in the recent work of Steven Marcus and J. Hillis Miller. It is not surprising that the early Dickens, perhaps the Dickens freest in spirit, should be first in their concern, as expressed in two recent essays which it will now be useful to consider.

In "Language into Structure: Pickwick Revisited," Marcus notes, referring to the famous double-talk of the opening chapter, that the "Pickwickian" sense of a word should be taken to mean

that sense in which the word is seized creatively in the first instance almost as a kind of doodle, as a play of the pen, as a kind of verbal scribble or game. It is the word—or verbal expression—actively regarded not primarily as conscious imitation of either nature or preexistent models, but rather as largely unconscious invention, whose meaning is created essentially as it is spontaneously uttered or written down.[7]

It is the flow of writing or spontaneous utterance in continuation that Marcus seizes upon as itself the structure of the book that follows, a "constant succession" (a phrase from Dickens' preface) "of language or writing in constant motion, moving itself."[8] Marcus intends that sense, both broader and more objective than the epithet

"Dickensian," in which Dickens' language is not an attribute but the very substance of his literary performance. The priority of language over such concepts as plot and imagination, from this point of view, is quite clear. Language is not merely or "primarily" the medium through which what is plotted or imagined is communicated, for, as Marcus has it, the language of *Pickwick Papers* exists in and for itself, "not primarily as conscious imitation" of something else. Not realism, but referentiality, is in question. How sweeping are the issues at stake is suggested by J. Hillis Miller at the beginning of his article on *Sketches by Boz* and *Oliver Twist,* "The Fiction of Realism":

> One important aspect of current literary criticism is the disintegration of the paradigms of realism under the impact of structural linguistics and the renewal of rhetoric. If meaning in language rises not from the reference of signs to something outside words but from differential relations among the words themselves, if "referent" and "meaning" must always be distinguished, then the notion of a literary text which is validated by its one-to-one correspondence to some social, historical, or pyschological reality can no longer be taken for granted. No language is purely mimetic or referential, not even the most utilitarian speech. The specifically literary form of language, however, may be defined as a structure of words which in one way or another calls attention to this fact, while at the same time allowing for its own inevitable misreading as a "mirroring of reality."[9]

Marcus quarrels with the view of literary language as "conscious imitation of nature or preexistent models"; Miller extends this to quarrel with those who would define realism—Watt has been my example—as the "faithful" representation of non-linguistic reality in a literary

text. However, Miller is far from providing a simple formulation of literature as self-referentiality. He is at pains
to avoid what he calls the "traditional polarity between
seeing literature as realistic representation, on the one
hand, and seeing it, on the other, as the creation of a self-
contained subjective realm. The view of literary language
I am presupposing would not see a work of literature as
able ever to be self-contained, self-sustaining, herme-
tically sealed in its self-referential purity." Thus it is crucial for Miller's theory that, although the primary task of
literary language is "to call attention to" "the set of language toward itself,"[10] the text still "allow[s] for its own
misreading" as representation.

The discussion of realism and the novel form in the
foregoing chapters will be understood as concurring in
the emphasis of Marcus and Miller in an important respect. The "mirroring of reality" in the text cannot, I
have been saying, be "taken for granted," and it is anything but taken for granted by the realist. Indeed, the
failure of literature to represent faithfully the real is the
defining preoccupation of realism. What I have described
as the consequence of this preoccupation, however,
makes clear the extent of my difference from these critics.
For the novelist's preoccupation with the novel's failure
of mimesis inevitably finds expression in the novel's
form, which is, then, the form of frustration. Thus the
mimetic intention, albeit in defeat, is yet formative of the
work. For Marcus and for Miller, the representational
task is less of a pressure upon the work, less consequen-
tial. They relegate to it a secondary importance, while
placing primary importance on another function which,
significantly, language *can satisfactorily perform:* for

Miller, the "correct" function of referring to itself as against the inevitable but "mistaken" referential or mimetic function; [11] for Marcus, language in free play, relieved of mimetic purposes. By placing primary importance on functions in which the use of language is successful, Marcus and Miller repudiate implicitly the importance of what I have just called frustration, the failed but attempted action of language against its own nature which is constitutive of the realist's distinctive linguistic usage.

Marcus' tribute to the language of *Pickwick Papers* as "wild" and "free" returns us to the recognition that with the issue of literary language's self-referentiality Dickens' celebratory tone is intrinsically bound up. But the relationship is extraordinarily difficult to describe. It has to do with the freeing of language from that task of extra-referentiality which, after all, it can only partially and imperfectly perform, for it is only then that the play of language upon itself can begin. Obviously it is wrong, however, to take a sequential view of the matter. Marcus insists that the language of *Pickwick* is free "in the first instance," and denies explicitly that it is "primarily" or first of all intended to denote a non-linguistic reality. But we have seen that the language of a passage in *Dombey* simultaneously elaborates its own trope playfully and sets before us an "iron-grey autumnal" vision of a man in his study. If there is not a point in time at which the language is suddenly freed from representation, nor, to be sure, a subsequent point at which language is wholly free, there is nonetheless a discernible simultaneous activity of language "beyond" its representational effort.

The complex differentiation of linguistic tone and

meaning in *Dombey* will recall a previous example of such contradictoriness, the mirror in the Veneerings' dining room. The metaphorical implications of the mirror brought out by Charley Hexam's arrival put in question the mimetic veracity of language, thus disobliging the language, as it were, of its mimetic effort, and unloosing what was described earlier as a romp of figurative language, which Marcus would be right in characterizing as "wild" and "free." But set against this wholehearted exploitation of linguistic device and necessarily issuing from some efficacious representation of the scene at the Veneerings is a content of considerable sociological and psychological interest, and, more, a portent of judgment morally serious and even severe. Charley's intrusion shows that the exclusion of his world by the Veneerings is culpable and "Podsnappish." His example involves the novel in a condemnation of its own excluding form, its inherent representational limits. Obviously, then, the mimetic responsibility of which the language has been partially disobliged is still making itself felt. But if not upon the language, then where? To answer, we must posit some broader structure of the work, untidily defined by the very contradictions that are before us, contradictions between form and language, meaning and tone. We must posit a heterogeneous structure "denoted," certainly, by language, but from which language is curiously independent, and vice versa.

Here, then, is a substantive way of distinguishing between Dickens' language and his "art." It is a consequence, it is important to see, of his valorization of the real world outside his novels, and of the mimetic task. The force of the mimetic imperative that art should copy the real is felt most decisively when its impossibility is also acknowledged, for then its effect is nothing less than the disintegration of the text, a meaningful disintegration into the contradictory matrix described above. But perhaps "disintegration" is too negative a term for the way in which the realist novel shares in and affirms life's own abundance of inconsistency and contradiction.

2

Chapter Three of *Little Dorrit*, "Home," begins by describing "a Sunday evening in London, gloomy, close, and stale":

Maddening church bells of all degrees of dissonance, sharp and flat, cracked and clear, fast and slow, made the brick-and-mortar echoes hideous. Melancholy streets, in a penitential garb of soot, steeped the souls of the people who were condemned to look at them out of windows, in dire despondency. In every thoroughfare, up almost every alley, and down almost every turning, some doleful bell was throbbing, jerking, tolling, as if the plague were in the city and the dead-carts were going round.   (I, iii, 67)

Arthur Clennam has just returned to this dismal scene after an absence of twenty years. Before taking himself to his mother's house, he pauses in a particularly dreary neighborhood:

Fifty thousand lairs surrounded him where people lived so unwholesomely that water put into their crowded rooms on Saturday night, would be corrupt on Sunday morning . . . Miles of close wells and pits of houses, where the inhabitants gasped for air, stretched far away towards every point of the compass. Through the heart of the town a deadly sewer ebbed and flowed, in the place of a fine fresh river. What secular

want could the million or so of human beings whose daily
labour, six days in the week, lay among these Arcadian
objects, from the sweet sameness of which they had no escape
between the cradle and the grave—what secular want could
they possibly have upon their seventh day? Clearly they could
want nothing but a stringent policeman.   (I, iii, 68)

The language of this chapter is deservedly well-known
among instances of Dickens' style in the late, "dark"
masterpieces. The passage, we note, turns from description to protest, bitterly sarcastic in tone, against those
who support the ban on Sunday amusements. But so earnest and impressive is Dickens in deploring what he describes that the shift seems a natural extension of the
description rather than a sudden topical aside; indeed,
by the date of the composition of *Little Dorrit* it was no
longer topical.[12] But the protest and the description par-
ticipate in each other. Just as our sense of the actual
"deadly sewer" is intensified by the mention of an imaginary "fine fresh river," the entrapment of the gasping
inhabitants is set off the more clearly by an evocation of
the release denied them on their day of rest, an effect
which is developed further by Dickens' specifications of
possible diversions: "No pictures, no unfamiliar animals,
no rare plants or flowers, no natural or artificial wonders
of the ancient world—all *taboo* with that enlightened
strictness, that the ugly South Sea gods in the British Mu-
seum might have supposed themselves at home again"
(I, iii, 67).

     This last citation is made to show the precise integra-
tion of the effects of protest and description, but it also
contains hints of a broader, more complex integration.
The "enlightened strictness" by which the alien gods are

to know they are "at home again" is an anticipation of the atmosphere of Mrs. Clennam's house, the "Home" of the chapter's title, which is pervaded by the oppressive spirit of her strict and fanatical religious devotion. By this anticipation the reader is being prepared for the revelation of Clennam's own inmost character, which directly follows the paragraphs of protest and description. When it comes, it takes striking form:

> Mr. Arthur Clennam sat in the window of the coffee-house on Ludgate Hill, counting one of the neighbouring bells, making sentences and burdens of songs out of it in spite of himself, and wondering how many sick people it might be the death of in the course of the year. As the hour approached, its changes of measure made it more and more exasperating. At the quarter, it went off into a condition of deadly-lively importunity, urging the populace in a voluble manner to Come to church, Come to church, Come to church! At the ten minutes, it became aware that the congregation would be scanty, and slowly hammered out in low spirits, They *won't* come, they *won't* come, they *won't* come! At the five minutes, it abandoned hope, and shook every house in the neighbourhood for three hundred seconds, with one dismal swing per second, as a groan of despair.
> "Thank Heaven!" said Clennam, when the hour struck, and the bell stopped.
> But its sound had revived a long train of miserable Sundays, and the procession would not stop with the bell, but continued to march on. "Heaven forgive me," said he, "and those who trained me. How I have hated this day!"
> (I, iii, 68–69)

For the speaking bell, too, the reader has been prepared. "Maddening church bells of all degrees of dissonance" are the first detail given in the description of London, and the "occasional jangling of discordant church bells" is the last detail given in the description of Marseilles, "broiling in the sun one day," that opens the novel. Such conspicuous mention alerts us to the importance of the bells, and of what they may be saying if their "dissonance" and "discord" be once sorted out. That the bell speaks at all, however, is a conceit of Clennam's, in which the narrator chooses to share, after making the attribution in significant language: Clennam is "counting one of the neighbouring bells, making sentences and burdens of song out of it in spite of himself."

Why "in spite of himself?" It will not do to recall, as one may, Mr. Chick's whistling at the Dombey christening. Not only is the scene here one of unremitting gloom, but Clennam himself, unlike Chick, is as morose as his surroundings. Clennam is depressive at most times, and at this particular moment he is anxious with special cause. By contrast to his mood, his making up of words from the monotonous tolling of the bell has about it something fanciful, playful, even frivolous. But in fact his conceit is intimately related to his emotional state, both in form and content. For one thing, the messages of the bell, "Come to church!" and "They won't come!", reflect the source of his present anxiety. It is he who won't come to the church of his mother's stern religion. Furthermore, he is bringing to his mother the unwelcome news that he has abandoned the family business, and, although he has always resisted her religious teaching, this is the first time by his own account that he has opposed her will. The difficulty of his imminent assertion of independence appears, obliquely, in the relief with which he hears that the hour is struck and the exhortation of the bell has stopped: "Thank Heaven!" Clearly the "burden" of the song he makes of the tolling is, in fact, his own burden of guilt. The same disposition to guilt, instilled in him as a child, will appear in the oppressive sense he later describes of some hidden wrongdoing in his father's past which it is his own duty to set right. Thus, in one sense, rather than being "in spite of" Clennam's state of mind, the words he "hears" in the bells do much to express it. And rather than contradicting Dickens' presentation of the character's psychology, the words provide or coroborate insight into his troubled childhood, his history of guilt and repression.

Not only the words, but also the fanciful turn of mind capable of such play is a part of Clennam's characterization. Later on, at the end of the chapter, it is explicitly related to the same psychological background. Concerning the paradox by which Clennam occasionally "soar[s] out of his gloomy life into the bright glories of fancy," we are told that "it had been the uniform tendency of this man's life—so much was wanting in it to think about, so much that might have been better directed and happier to speculate upon—to make him a dreamer after all" (i, iii, 80).

There is an interesting dialectical aspect to this explanation for the evolution of dreamer out of repressed child, and it bears directly on the novel's ubiquitous concern with freedom, with jails and escape, oppression and liberation. What is suggested is that the mind's instinct for freedom is finally irresistible, and if the mind is denied "happy" occasions for speculation in real life, it will turn naturally to a habit of unreality. In this particular instance and in others, Dickens establishes a fine and difficult correlation between the mind's unreal improvisations and the reality it confronts. Clennam's game is the result of a semiconscious but also a profoundly open reception of the sound he hears. During the tolling of the bell, he is abstracted, and his inner state is relatively exposed, unguarded, so that the sounds enter and mingle at the deepest level with the themes of his introspection, as his subsequent conversation with the waiter reveals:

> "Beg pardon, sir," said a brisk waiter, rubbing the table. "Wish see bedroom?"
>
> "Yes I have just made up my mind to do it."
>
> "Chaymaid!" cried the waiter . . .
>
> "Stay!" said Clennam, rousing himself. "I was not thinking of what I said; I answered mechanically. I am not going to sleep here. I am going home.   (I, iii, 69–70)

His first response is somnambulistic, an out-loud revelation of his meditation, summoned by the half-comprehended question of the waiter. I have said that the balance Dickens achieves is fine and difficult, because the mind is shown to be, at such times, neither wholly independent of present reality nor wholly contingent upon it or dominated by it. Nor, indeed, is the mind presented as wholly adjusted to some midpoint between freedom and contingency. Clennam must reverse his answer to the waiter, must contradict himself. His condition of mind is self-contradictory in the fullest measure.

With this we come near to unpacking the significance of the narrator's remark that Clennam plays his word game with the bells "in spite of himself." Both the words he makes up and the inclination to do so can be explained in psychological terms, by reference to the nexus of represion and disappointment that has been his life. But at the logical crux of that explanation is a rever-

sal, a contradiction. He plays because he has been oppressed, he expresses his freedom because he has been
denied it. In fact, as an activity of fancy Clennam's little
word game is a kind of liberation, a release like that
which Dickens tells us the prisoners of the city are themselves in need of on a Sunday. But one should be conscious of irony in speaking of an "activity of fancy" as a
liberation while admitting that its form and content have
been psychologically determined.

Clennam's is, specifically, a linguistic liberation, and
its implications for Dickens' over-arching linguistic project in the novel are considerable. They seem especially
worth taking up because there is that in the writing of
Chapter Three of *Dorrit* which calls attention to an analogy between Dickens' activity and Clennam's. Clennam,
we know, is filling in with words a series of sounds he is
hearing, but the filling in does not stop when the sound
ceases. The series "had revived a long train of miserable
Sundays, and the procession would not stop with the
bell, but continued to march on." There follows a paragraph whose parallelism suggests a continuation within
Clennam of the rhythm of the silent bell:

> There was the dreary Sunday of his childhood, when he
> sat with his hands before him, scared out of his senses . . .
> There was the sleepy Sunday of his boyhood, when, like a
> military deserter, he was marched to chapel . . . There was
> the interminable Sunday of his nonage . . . There was the
> resentful Sunday of a little later . . .   (I, iii, 69)

And so forth. Parallelism, strongly rhythmic, for the use
of which the novel as a whole is conspicuous, marks the
writing in the third chapter from its beginning:

No pictures, no unfamiliar animals, no rare plants or flowers, no artificial wonders . . . Nothing to see but streets, streets, streets. Nothing to breathe but streets, streets, streets. Nothing to change the brooding mind, or raise it up. Nothing for the spent toiler to do . . .   (I, iii, 67)

Versification is only the clearest case of what is true of any rhythmic, repetitive structure of words, that it sets up in the ear the expectation of a pattern of stresses, which are to be filled in by words. Thus Dickens, in the present case, fills in with words a "pre-existing" rhythmic pattern, as Clennam fills in the strokes of the bell. The content provided by Dickens is not gratuitous, of course, any more than the words Clennam chooses are irrelevant to his character or psychological background. Neither is the form of parallelism an arbitrary one: The narrator, as we have already observed, mentions church bells prominently before Clennam is said to hear them, and their rhythmic tolling, as echoed in the language, contributes to the mood of the description. We may say, in fact, that Dickens' use of language in the opening pages of the chapter is determined by purposes of mimesis or representation. The content is representational. Protest and description reinforce one another to give a vivid impression of the scene. The form is, precisely, mimetic. It imitates in its rhythm, in its parallel grammatical structure, in the low-pitched and narrow-mouthed vocables it employs, the monotonous sound of the tolling of the church bells "really there" in gloomy London that evening.

But it is clear, too, that Dickens' use of language here partakes of the paradoxical quality of liberation that has been attributed to Clennam's above. The reader can be aware of the strict representational utility of every linguistic detail of the writing, the subtle integrity of effect and mutualities of meaning. But if he returns to the beginning of Chapter Three and reads through, he will be struck again, when he returns to Clennam's game of wording the bell, by a faint but distinct inappropriateness of tone, on Dickens' part as well as on Clennam's. The spirit in which it is conceived and executed is more indulgent, seemingly freer—in Marcus' sense, more "Pickwickian"—than the language of the humorless depiction of the dismal city or the angry sarcasm toward its lawmakers, or the language, which follows, of the gloomy meditation on past Sundays. The reader will feel that a linguistic idea attractive and pleasing in itself is being indulged here—indulged, as it were, on the Sabbath, in spite of the spiritual lawmakers—although its indulgence creates a sudden dissonance, discernible if not "jangling," in the tone of the exposition. The form Dickens gives to the indulgence of fancy he has allowed himself, and the contents with which he endows it, are intimately related to and expressive of his purposes in the scene. But not quite obscured by such evident utility is the impression of an urge, local, temporary, and divergent, to play a game with words for its own sake. Something like what was identified in the passage from *Dombey* as a distance between tone and meaning is again in evidence. The reader cannot say of this or that detail that it is nonrepresentational or autonomous, but he can recognize, nonetheless, the creative accents of language exercising and enjoying an authentic if almost invisible freedom to be itself.

The real interest of the analogy between Dickens'

"liberated" indulgence of a linguistic fancy, on one hand, and Clennam's, on the other, lies in the dialectical explanation given in the text for the latter. Clennam was inclined to a habit of dreaming unreality, it is said, because of the oppressiveness of his waking world. The world as it is represented in *Little Dorrit,* critics have agreed widely, deserves such shunning. It nearly deserves to be characterized by Wilson's phrase, as a "prison of life." It is tempting to apply the dialectical formula forthwith to Dickens' linguistic play, and say that his language recoiled from an unremitting portrayal of that bleak world, and sought release in an occasional outburst, a mild one such as the imagination of the speaking bells, or more elaborate and extended ones, such as Flora Finching's monologues, or Mrs. Plornish's redoubtable "Tuscan."

The general argument I have been developing, however, suggests a different explanation, which will need testing. It is that language is oppressed, not by the grimness of the prison-like world it represents in *Little Dorrit* or elsewhere, but by the prison-like exigencies of representation itself. Dickens' sudden linguistic indulgence is a gesture which has an aspect of escape. I have been saying that Dickens is one of the company of realists, because the form of his novels protests against their confinement and distortion of reality. It should be added that he is also that artist of language in love with his medium, whose use of words protests against the limitations imposed upon them in the service of representational form. In establishing the first of these claims, I focused upon the realist's protest against the fact of closure inseparable from the idea of form. The second involves the artist's protest against the stricture of internal

uniformity or consistency which is also a feature of the
formalist conception of the nature of a literary text.

It is worth pausing here to remark that consistency
was really the hidden term of value in that tidy dichot-
omy of "coherence" versus "correspondence" which
begged more than its share of questions in the New Critical heyday. The relative fuzziness of the pair will account for the relief one probably feels in turning to the
plainspoken formula with which W. K. Wimsatt climaxes
a history of literary criticism: Poetry's "special character," according to Wimsatt, is a "tensional union of making with seeing and saying." [13] "Making" for coherence,
"seeing and saying" for correspondence. The improvement is visible. "Coherence," especially, is clarified by
being deprived of its double meaning in general usage,
by which it silently suggests that only texts marked by a
distinct "coherence" of parts (each to each, within the
whole) are "coherent" *qua* intelligible. But Wimsatt does
not finally alter the usual New Critical priority of "coherential" over "correspondential" values, for the figure
"tensional union" is itself borrowed from the physical
world of "making" or of made things. The figure implies
a harmony and cooperation, suggestibly a balance of opposite stresses which holds the artifact intact. The kind of
"both-and"-ness which Cleanth Brooks in *The Well-
Wrought Urn* means by paradox is an example of a con-
structive opposition of the elements of meaning, rather
than rank contradictoriness and incommensurateness
among the parts. [14] Even in the most supple work of the
formalists, then, there is a (quite intentional) bias toward
the text as artifact.

A review of this body of assumptions has particular

relevance here in light of the history of the reputation of
the text at hand. In 1953, Lionel Trilling was able to remark that, of the novels of Dickens' "great last period,"
Little Dorrit was "the least established with modern readers." But he said so at the beginning of an essay on the
novel that was to do a great deal toward establishing its
present eminence. And it is interesting that, although
Trilling is rarely named among the New Critics who are
his contemporaries, the central of several lines of argument in the essay follows the formalist predilection for
"coherence," complex, precise, and systematic integrity
of structure. He stresses Dickens' tightness of control, the
aegis of "conscious intention rather than . . . free creation" under which the book is written. "We do not have
the great population of characters from whom shines the
freshness of their autonomous life," as in earlier Dickens
novels. Instead, we find "an imagination under the dominion of a great articulated idea." In his use of the language of "autonomy" and "dominion," however, there is
an apparently unsuspected paradox. The "great articulated idea" is the novel's profound analysis of society,
and Trilling focuses upon the prison imagery which is its
negative symbol. But at the same time he describes with
admiration the operation of Dickens' creative powers in
terms of imprisonment: the absence of "autonomous
life," the subjugation to "abstraction," to an "idea." Indeed, his influential notion of the success of the novel's
symbolism turns on his perception of a further structural
imprisonment. Although he begins by saying the novel's
prison imagery is effective because "the prison is an actuality before it is ever a symbol," he eventually notes
approvingly that images surrender their actuality as they

take on their symbolic function in the novel as a whole: "This novel at its best is only incidentally realistic; its finest power of imagination appears in the great general images whose abstractness is their actuality."[15] How it can be that a novel which voices the themes of its moral concern in a veritable hymn to independence should take for itself so Bastille-like a version of aesthetic form, Trilling does not say. But the opinion is still current that *Little Dorrit* is one of the best integrated, controlled, or "organized" of Dickens' novels, and this is a cornerstone of the novel's high repute.

It would be frustrating, this account of *Dorrit*'s virtues notwithstanding, to attempt to apply the artifactual view of a text, with its standards of closure and consistency, uniformity and homogeneity, to the small but significant contradictions we have noted in Chapter Three of *Little Dorrit,* or in the passage from *Dombey.* To do so, one would have to use the already conceded representational justification of each detail not so much to explain as to "explain away" such tonal dissonances—to explain, indeed, that they were really harmonies and "tensional unions." What is special and unusual about the contradictions revealed in these examples, it is well to remember, is their momentary explicitness only. They "indulge" or "celebrate" a real but evanescent condition of freedom that inheres in language at all times, although it rarely, and never quite, announces itself.

Moreover, such instances have a distributive effect, making visible the hidden capacity for autonomy in the apparently unfree language of the surrounding text. This effect resembles one noted in an earlier chapter. In the discussion of *War and Peace,* two passages were contrasted, one of seemingly greater contingency than the other, that is, more dependent for its meaning on participation in the novel as a whole. I noted that the awareness of relative independence in one passage has a liberating effect on the reading of the other. We become aware of the capacity of both for other than "coherential" significance. Under the influence of such an effect in *Little Dorrit*, we will be little inclined to agree with Trilling in his praise for the seamless confluence of the actual and symbolic, or the penultimate absorption and disappearance of the actual into the symbolic. We will want, rather, to respond fully to the actuality of the book's descriptions— of the Marshalsea, of Sunday on Ludgate Hill, of Venice. We will want, of course, to apprehend and "interpret" the function of such descriptions in the novel's symbolic or imaginative pattern, but at the same time we will not permit such apprehension to mitigate or etiolate our other, immediate and local response to the prison as prison, the fog as fog.

The linguistic, tonal contradictions in Chapter Three of the novel follow the form of such simultaneous but separate affectivity. The protest against the strict Sunday ordinances can be intelligently and usefully related to the chapter's organizing subject, Clennam's "Home," but it also asserts locally the force of what, after all, it really is: an angry complaint against those laws in the London of those days. The passage has a valence both inward and outward. By one of its implications, modern lawmakers of a similar frame of mind are indicted; by another, as we have seen, Mrs. Clennam is. But before it implies or connects with anything, the language engages the reader with itself directly and intensely in a self-defining way.

The greatly paradoxical consequence of this argument has perhaps already been suggested by the mention of *War and Peace*, of *Dorrit*'s Marshalsea and its strain of social protests, or perhaps especially by the mention of the "actuality" that can escape the "imprisonment" of symbolic context. This consequence is that what Robert Gorham Davis calls "the sense of the real" in fiction has perhaps most to gain from the recognition of the incomplete determinancy, the incremental freedom, of literary language.[16] For the legitimate inconsistency of the text, in which this freedom of language is located, means that the text can (partially, imperfectly) represent the object of its interest in the real world without necessarily confining or reducing it. To some extent, that is, it can represent and *let stand* a chosen piece of the real, without having to assimilate all its multitude of relevant and irrelevant attributes and associations into the uniform fabric of the contextual whole. And the independence of the object of representation, in which its impress of actuality subsists, is in fact guaranteed by the coexistence of mimetic or descriptive uses of language with its other modes and uses in the text.

3

That the inconsistency of a text stands behind or legitimates its realism receives a curiously direct exposition in Chapter One of *The Old Curiosity Shop*. Master Humphrey has returned home after his bewildering encounter with Little Nell and her grandfather and finds he cannot dismiss from his thoughts the image of the little girl, "so very young, so spiritual, so slight and fairy-like a creature passing the long dull nights in such an uncongenial place." Then he announces the theory that it is the uncongeniality of the place that is in fact responsible for the persistence of the image, the deep impression of her memory: ·

> We are so much in the habit of allowing impressions to be made upon us by external objects, which should be produced by reflection alone, but which, without such visible aids, often escape us; that I am not sure I should have been so thoroughly possessed by this one subject, but for the heaps of fantastic things I had seen huddled together in the curiosity-dealer's warehouse. These, crowding upon my mind, in connection with the child, and gathering round her, as it were, brought her condition palpably before me. I had her image, without any effort of imagination, surrounded and beset by everything that was foreign to its nature, and furthest removed from the sympathies of her sex and age. If these helps to my fancy had all been wanting, and I had been forced to imagine her in a common chamber, with nothing unusual or uncouth in its appearance, it is very probable that I should have been less impressed with her strange and solitary state. As it was, she seemed to exist in a kind of allegory; and having these shapes about her, claimed my interest so strongly, that (as I have already remarked) I could not dismiss her from my recollection, do what I would.   (i, 55–56)

The paradox gains momentum as the paragraph proceeds. His sense of her is intensely true and real. Her "condition" is "palpably before" him undistorted by "any effort of imagination." But the deep and, it turns out, deeply right impression of her "strange and solitary state" is produced in him precisely by the irrelevance, the foreignness to her nature, of the scene in which she is presented. He would not have been so deeply aware of her if he had encountered her "in a common chamber"—

that is, in the room that might have been chosen as the right one for her, the typical or "realistic" setting that might have been provided by Defoe or perhaps Zola. What Dickens argues here, through the words of Master Humphrey, as he argues in Mr. Venus' workshop and from the rocking chair of Jenny Wren, is that the verisimilitudinous is not the realistic. The real is only apprehended by art where its actuality is not diminished or swallowed up by a tedious exactitude of imitation, a tediously reasoned appropriateness of context. Something essential to the Dickensian representation of reality, I think, reveals itself in Master Humphrey's words, and we are not greatly wrong if we are reminded by it of Marianne Moore's metaphor for one relation of art to reality, "imaginary gardens with real toads in them," or of Lionel Trilling's incisive rejoinder to it: "Indeed, we have come to believe that the toad is the less real when the garden is also real." [17]

It has been said that the portrait of Dombey in his library is metonymic. He shares in the nature of the objects which literally (in the text) constitute his usual environment, and he can be described by describing them. This substitution of proximate things is what metonymy means, of course, but the form of the scene as a whole, clearly, is that of a satirical metaphor. In Master Humphrey's terms, it is "a kind of allegory," in which objects—the bust of Pitt, the pulpit-like urns, Dombey himself—stand for entities in the real world, adding up to a model of that smug bourgeois prosperity which is the real object, in both senses, of Dickens' satire. Thus the relationship among chosen details is metonymic, but their aggregate form is metaphoric or allegorical. In a way, just the reverse obtains in the portrait of Nell in the lumber room of the Old Curiosity Shop. Between Nell and the objects that surround her there are no links. If there is a logic to their proximity, it is external to their real condition, their perceptible surfaces, unlike the "stiff and stark" fire-irons which resemble their owner. It is this that Master Humphrey means by saying that Nell *"seemed to* exist in a kind of allegory" (emphasis added), for in allegory the logic of proximity can only be understood by reference to some undisclosed, external code. Thus the presentation of the surface of the scene resembles allegory in the ostensibly arbitrary heaping of things, with the difference that in fact there is no undisclosed, external code. As the novel elaborately testifies, the alienation of Nell from what surrounds her is genuine.

The impression of arbitrary heaping or accumulation, the regnant inconsistency of context, through which the real and individual image of Nell exerts its effect without distortion, is finally to be explained with reference to the metonymic, rather than allegorical-metaphoric, structure of the scene. The realist novel, I have said, does not so much metaphorically substitute its world for the real world as mark off "with imperfect closure . . . a certain area of experience actually located on the world's horizon." Thus its form is that of a fragment rather than a whole, and the principle governing "relevance" or inclusion in the fragment is that of the lumber room: "mere" contiguity. It is only in the one-to-one analogical relations of metaphor that the inclusion of a given particular may be pressed for causality and significance, coherence and correspondence.

Nell's reality is the undisturbed randomness of her situation. As surrogate for the reader, Master Humphrey is alive to her actuality because her "strange" and unreal setting has denied him that systematic understanding which is prologue to dismissing her from thought. In this there is an important clue to the method of Dickens' art generally. To understand Nell is to lose her image. Imagination, it seems, does less harm than reason to the reality it apprehends. In the inconstancy and jumble of the lumber room, a light is thrown on the complex and multitudinous coexistence of real and imaginary, likely and fantastical, in Dickens' art, and on how it is that the impress of actuality survives amid the abundance of what is bizarre, grotesque, and impossible.

These latter asseverations concern the contradictoriness and inconsistency of the denoted or "signified" world of the novels. The real and the imaginary are separately and together the referents of Dickens' language, and their simultaneity is not untroubled. What I have tried to say is that at least one consequence of their simultaneity and interaction is the intensification of our response to the real. But the present chapter began with a consideration of inconsistencies of another order, linguistic and tonal, which imply the simultaneity and separateness of the referential and self-reflexive functions of language. And here, too, the first consequence is a more direct and immediate response to the material, and a diminution of responses that are processed through a contingent, contextual understanding of the text. Again our sense of the actual is the beneficiary. It is intensified and exacerbated by the awareness of contradiction.

We find repeatedly, in fact, that the adumbration of

inconsistency and contradiction by a metonymic structure is fundamental to the working out of the aims of realism. The reason is significant. The realist prefers
metonymic over metaphoric form because of his decisive
perception that indeed we do not experience the world as
a coherence of parts, bearing mutual significance in a
whole that emerges from the subtle compatibility of their
apparent contradictions. For Dickens, an art that can affirm only the life it can encompass and synthesize, can
therefore affirm life only at the expense of its reality. For
life's reality is a contradictoriness that is not equipoise
but schism, not harmony but a jangling discordance, as
of bells.

4. The Sentimental Criticism of Philosophy in *Oliver Twist*

In his article on *Pickwick Papers*, to which reference was made in the last chapter, Steven Marcus writes of the "framed tales" in the novel that they are constructed on

the obverse principle to that which informs the body of the novel. In them motion and movement of both language and event come to a dead halt. In almost every one of them, even the funny ones, someone is paralyzed, immobilized or locked up, and imprisoned in something. Their language is not the free, wild, astonishingly creative language of the balance of the novel. It tends almost uniformly to be obsessed, imprisoned, anal, caught in various immobile repetitive modes. [1]

Even apart from its periodic confinement in the framed tales, the "free, wild" language of the novel does not continue in an unrestrained outpouring through to the ending. Pickwick's term in the Fleet represents what Marcus calls an engagement of the limitations of that freedom actually celebrated in the rest of the novel, especially its social and economic limitations. And this is true, Marcus might have added, not only of the incarceration in the Fleet but also of the benevolent incarceration by Pickwick and Weller of themselves and their friends in the big house at Dulwich, where their adventures come to a close.

Of the penultimate confinement, Marcus somewhat cryptically remarks that Dickens' "entire future development is contained by anticipation in that nullification."[2] Perhaps he is thinking of the mood of incarceration of the novel which was to follow. *Oliver Twist* has been characterized by a remarkable diversity of critics as "closed" and "claustral," an "imaginative complex of claustrophobia."[3] It is as if critics were obscurely compelled by the novel's mood to describe it in words beginning with the threatening curve of the letter "c," about to close its jaws. As with the Fleet and Dulwich, both the "bad" and "good" worlds of the novel are rendered in an atmosphere of confinement. That is, the "little society" of Brownlow and the Maylies, which is a safe, snug haven to Oliver probably strikes most of us, no less than Fagin's den, as insufferably close. The terrible claustrophobia of the novel's landscape has been often and expertly described: the inward, kaleidoscopic proliferation of crowded streets, small rooms, narrow staircases, dark nooks and crannies.

But what is claustral about Dickens' second novel is not limited to its topography. It is one of the three or four of his novels—*Hard Times* and *Little Dorrit* are others— that are praised for the tightness of their construction, the smooth and revelatory inter-relatedness of parts. Sylvère Monod is able to object strongly to "digressions" in

Oliver Twist he would perforce accept in *Pickwick* because they stand out more clearly against the more closely-knit fabric of the later novel, a fabric, moreover, which reveals openly the pattern of its manufacture.[4] The carefully calibrated opposition of the commercial middle class and the criminal underworld—borrowed, it is sometimes said, from *The Beggar's Opera*—is only the most obvious way in which Oliver Twist gives the impression of having been thrown open to the public with its scaffolding still in place. It is a novel which encourages by the transparency of its planning quasi-allegorical interpretations and interpretation by schema.

This encouragement is not flatly to be resisted, and it will be yielded to shortly, but first it is necessary to take note of a paradox akin to one I have touched upon earlier in reference to *Little Dorrit*. If the form the novel takes is claustral, so also is the form of what the novel attacks: the imprisonment of Oliver's spirit, the negation of his freedom. And claustral, too, it has just been said, is the world of the novel's good people, the world the novel values for its (claustral) values of hearth and home, warmth and security.

Oliver Twist is a novel famous for thrilling us with its portraits of evil and boring us with its portraits of good. We are right to object to what is simple-minded and meretricious in the latter, although we should not miss that the decisive disproportion of entertainment values between evil and good thinly masks a compliment from the former to the latter. Evil we can more easily take the measure of; virtue, especially our own, is mysterious. Milton's God is perhaps infelicitously rendered in part because Milton held that he is unfathomable, and therefore declines the pretense of fathoming him. Caliban engages us more vivaciously and intensely than Miranda, but in the latter there is a tantalizing essence dancing just beyond our grasp—and Shakespeare-Prospero's. Such allusions cannot dispel what is finally annoying about Oliver's shadowy innocence. We do not explain a thing by saying it is a mystery. Nor is it quite enough, although it is something, to point out that the novel does not endorse Rose Maylie's pale virtue so persuasively as it demonstrates the difficult and self-defeating goodness of Nancy. Rather, the style and quality of feeling that is called "sentimental" must itself be brought into the light. And when the judgment, which no one will hesitate to make, against the insufficiency of such feeling has been registered, it is yet not impossible to discover that the very shadowiness that constitutes the offense has for its cause an unwillingness to trap or confine the real force of good, and that that unwillingness can itself be honored as intelligent and realistic. Dickens' renditions of goodness may be, as George Eliot said they were, "transcendent in [their] unreality," but his reluctance to give goodness too known or knowable a form is consistent with the realistic principle informing Dickens' work more or less throughout: that the reality of a thing is its freedom. The prospects for this finding are good enough to encourage investigation, schematic, as the novel dictates, at least at the start.

2

That when the Dodger, and his accomplished friend Master Bates, joined in the hue-and-cry which was raised at Oliver's heels in consequence of their executing illegal

conveyance of Mr. Brownlow's personal property, as has
already been described, they were actuated by a very laudable
and becoming regard for themselves; and forasmuch as the
freedom of the subject and the liberty of the individual are
among the first and proudest boasts of a true-hearted
Englishman; so, I need hardly beg the reader to observe, that
this action should tend to exalt them in the opinion of all
public and patriotic men; in almost as great a degree as this
strong proof of their anxiety for their own preservation and
safety, goes to corroborate and confirm the little code of laws
which certain profound and sound-judging philosophers have
laid down as the mainsprings of all Nature's deeds and
actions: the said philosophers very wisely reducing the good
lady's proceedings to matters of maxim and theory: and, by a
very neat and pretty compliment to her exalted wisdom and
understanding, putting entirely out of sight any considerations
of heart, or generous impulse and feeling. For these are
matters totally beneath a female who is acknowledged by
universal admission to be far above the numerous little foibles
and weaknesses of her sex.   (xii, 73)

In the above, Dickens brings together conveniently a
set of terms crucial to the structure and meaning of his
novel. The conflict which emerges explicitly here between "philosophers," on the one hand, and "heart, or
generous impulse and feeling," and their advocates, on
the other, is one which underlies the novel at all points,
with rival and exclusive versions of "Nature" implied by
each. Once its thick and various layers of irony have
been sorted out, the paragraph contends with relative
directness that it is "philosophical" to act in a self-in-
terested manner, and to regard self-interest as one of the
first laws of nature. It follows as a "philosophical" corollary that nature is in fact reducible to laws. "Heart, or
generous impulse and feeling" refers, then, to what "phi-

losophers" leave out: concern for others, and "deeds and actions" prompted by such concern, founded not on considerations of "maxim and theory" but on "impulse." Implicit is a view of nature that is not abstract and theoretical but instinctive and suprarational.

The opposition is not, of course, stated impartially. The narrator, in his irony, quite openly connives at defining "philosophy" in such a way as to disparage it. And the definition is consistent with the frequent use of the word throughout the novel. By virtue of this consistency and frequency, what Dickens means by the "philosophical" turns out to be more easily discernible than what he means by "heart, or generous impulse and feeling." There is even a useful historical gloss on "philosophers." On one level, the term refers to the "Philosophical Radicals" of the *Westminster Review,* whose ideas were to be found just beneath the surface of the reform legislation of the 1830's, the subject of the novel's satire. The workhouse chapters, for example, have as their express target the Poor Law of 1834, which transformed some existing charitable institutions in a direction suggested by Utilitarian ideas.[5] One passage out of many will suffice to show how vociferous was Dickens' indignation against the philosophers who stood behind the offending institutions. Oliver, just come to the Sowerberries' from the workhouse, is given the dog's leftovers to eat:

I wish some well-fed philosopher whose meat and drink turn to gall within him; whose blood is ice, whose heart is iron; could have seen Oliver Twist clutching at the dainty viands that the dog had neglected. I wish he could have witnessed the horrible avidity with which Oliver tore the bits asunder

with all the ferocity of famine. There is only one thing I
should like better; and that would be to see the Philosopher
making the same sort of meal himself, with the same relish.
(iv, 24–25)

It would be a mistake to believe that this lively animus is
directed only against that handful of liberal thinkers and
social planners who directly influenced such matters as
the workhouse diet. The outrage, if not the issue, has a
more general significance. John Stuart Mill himself recognized that such criticism not only attacked his position,
but implied a certain position-taking of its own, and he
tried to say what that was: "We found all the opinions to
which we attached most importance, constantly attacked
on the ground of feeling. Utility was denounced as cold
calculation; political economy as hard-hearted; anti-
population doctrines as repulsive to the natural feelings
of mankind. We retorted by the word 'sentimentality'."[6]

Dickens' sentimentalism—a more fair-minded choice
of a word, I think, than Mill's—is ever that aspect of his
work least in favor, most neglected, and perhaps least
understood.[7] It also represents to most minds the readiest
objection to the case for Dickens' realism, although this
reaction is more instinctive than reasoned. Deeper than
axiomatic is our assumption, for example, that happy
endings are less realistic than sad ones, less even than so
melodramatic a piece of sadness as the end of *A Farewell
to Arms*. But the explanation for our resistance to Dickens' sentimentalism lies not only, although it does in
part, in the protective diffidence of our emotionally jaded
century. We do really suspect, as well, that the shadowy
realms of "heart, or generous impulse and feeling"—the
very phrase is indecisively reiterative—are ambiguous in

other than the celebrated modern sense: not complex and multivalent, but merely vaguely and insubstantially con-ceived. *Oliver Twist* offers an especially good opportunity for penetrating these shadows. In it, "heart" has at least a specific and discernible opposite, which Dickens calls "philosophy," and it has, moreover, what heart does not always seem to have, a function, as a stance for the criticism of its opposite. It ought to be possible to elucidate one term by means of the other, and, in so doing, to force from their opposition a maximum justifiable statement of the alternative views of "Nature" inherent in each, and of the nature and significance of Dickens' choice between them.

The passage I began by considering occurs at the beginning of Chapter Thirteen, a moment at which Oliver is safe in the "sentimental" refuge of Brownlow's house from the "philosophical" evils of two worlds, Fagin's den and the workhouse. Until this point in the book the term "philosopher" has been used only for persons associated with the Poor Law institutions. Now the conduct of the Dodger and Charley Bates is described as "strictly philosophical" because it is self-serving, just as Mrs. Mann, who operates the baby farm, shows herself to be "a very great experimental philosopher" by pocketing "the greater part of the weekly stipend" provided for maintenance of the farm (ii, 4). So also the board of the workhouse is described as "philosophical" shortly before it engages to sell Oliver to the murderous chimneysweep Gamfield for three pounds ten (iii).

Although broad, Dickens' satire here strikes deeply. Raymond Williams has shown that in attributing self-in-

terest to the Philosophical Radicals Dickens exposes a
contradiction in their philosophical program, although he
does so "not analytically," as Williams notes, "but in an
act of emotional and substantial recoil and revulsion":

When Dickens was writing, the utilitarian emphasis was a
compound of rationalism and *laissez-faire* economics, in spite
of the substantial contradiction between an appeal to general
utility and a recommendation of non-interference. [These
were] combined . . . by the urgent and over-riding interests
of a class . . . What he is then refuting is not so much an idea
as a whole social formation. The reliance on reason had been
cleansing and liberating, but as the instrument of a class
which was both reforming and aggressive it became, in a real
history, an alienation in which the calculation of interest was
separated from all other human impulses and ties.[8]

Ultimately, though, the calculation of self-interest,
especially where it is "separated from all other human
impulses and ties" (compare "heart, or generous impulse
and feeling") is associated with the novel's most remarkable philosophical character, Fagin himself. In a famous
scene, he tells a new pupil that every man is his own best
friend. "Some conjurers say that number three is the
magic number, and some say seven. It's neither, my
friend, neither. It's number one . . . meaning yourself"
(xliii, 293). It is interesting and important to notice that
this advice occurs in the course of an elaborate and
"philosophical" exchange in which Fagin seeks to con-
vince Noah Claypole of the value of the principle of trust
on which the club is founded. Effectively, it is a parody
of the social contract that underlies classical capitalism.
But it is also a parody of reasoned argument generally,
nearly two pages long, and ending with a resounding Q.

E. D.: "So we come at last to what I told you at first—that a regard for number one holds us all together, and must do so, unless we would all go to pieces in company" (xliii, 294).

Besides self-interest, Fagin shares with the world of official charity another "philosophical" attribute. He treats people like things. This aspect of life in the care of the parish, expressed memorably in the diction of the opening chapters, has often been noted.[9] Oliver is an "item of mortality" (i, 1), the "fact of a new burden" (i, 2), a "dead-weight, a millstone" (iv, 21), the very midwife at his birth is named Mrs. Thingummy. He is "badged and ticketed" like so much stuff (i, 3). He is a tool, to be shoved into small spaces, as Gamfield proposes to do, and as Sikes eventually does. He is "an article direct from the manufactory of the very devil himself" (iii, 13). To the parish he is worth a five-pound reward for removal. Later Monks will set a value on him of "hundreds of pounds," but the difference is merely one of price.

Treatment of a person as a thing is, in the novel's terms, "philosophical," in the sense of "reducing Nature's proceedings to matters of maxim and theory," and, again, "putting entirely out of sight any considerations of heart, or generous impulse and feeling." Although, as I have said, this cluster of sentimental terms is vague and general, here their meaning is a virtue of their generality, for in their indefiniteness they alert us to the "philosophical" error of too reductive, too confining, too thinglike a conception of the human individual. Here sentimentalism first reveals its participation in the protest against (aesthetic, psychological, linguistic) repression that we have seen to be fundamental to Dickens' purposes at all times, and that is founded in turn upon his distinctive realism, his perception of ultimate irrepressibility in the real. The "philosophical" here is, in fact, the claustral. It is the negation of what cannot be denominated or described other than vaguely, the denial of what resists our forms of knowing or understanding. As in the realist novel's tortuous indictment of itself, sentimentalism here surrenders to a necessary ineptitude of language in order to confess or signify, even if imperfectly, the reality and importance of what lies outside the capacities of linguistic formation. Such reality it is "philosophical," precisely, to dismiss.

This is near to the sense of the term as it is used in Chapter Seven, when Bumble is called in to quell the "owdacious murderer" Oliver at the Sowerberries'. The undertaker's wife suggests that Oliver, who has just attacked Noah Claypole with more than enough justification, is probably mad. But she is corrected by Bumble after a "few moments of deep meditation":

"It's not Madness, ma'am . . . it's Meat . . . You've overfed him, ma'am. You've raised a artificial soul and spirit in him, ma'am, unbecoming a person of his condition: as the board, Mrs. Sowerberry, who are practical philosophers, will tell you. What have paupers to do with soul or spirit? It's quite enough that we let 'em have live bodies." (vii, 41)

Good Mr. Brownlow houses and clothes and feeds Oliver just as Bumble and Fagin have done, but there is a more significant token of his generosity to distinguish him from Oliver's previous benefactors. The first conversation between Oliver and Brownlow is given to establishing his name (xii). He had been given the name

"Tom White" for convenience in court, out of total disregard for his real and unique identity. It is suggestive that the name Oliver Twist itself is an accident of the alphabet, as Bumble explains: Twist happened to be born, among nameless waifs, between Swubble and Unwin. Thus Oliver's very name is a symbol of his distorting (twisting?) reification at the hands of "philosophers," whereas the sentimental Mr. Brownlow, whose "heart" was "large enough for any six ordinary gentlemen," will restore Oliver to his true name and his real identity at last.

One of the arresting aspects of the sentimental criticism of philosophy in *Oliver Twist* is its anticipation in small of Marx's elaborate analysis of the treatment of people as things under capitalism, to which he applied the term "reification." The novel shows how those who treat others as objects become objects themselves. This retaliation—Dantean as well as Marxian—is already at work in the passage cited earlier, in which Oliver eats the dog's leftovers. In that place, the "philosopher" who has denied Oliver's humanity has himself blood of "ice," and a heart of "iron:" materials cold and hard and inorganic. The same effect obtains in the punning when Oliver, newly arrived in the workhouse, is informed

that the board had said he was to appear before it forthwith.
    Not having a very clearly defined notion of what a live board was, Oliver was rather astounded by this intelligence
. . .
    "Bow to the board," said Bumble. Oliver brushed away two or three tears . . . and seeing no board but the table, fortunately bowed to that.   (ii, 8)
He had been wondering, with his eyes fixed on the

magistrates' powder, whether all boards were born with that white stuff on their heads, and were boards from thenceforth on that account.   (III, 17)

Perhaps the most obvious form this self-reification takes in the novel is the distortion of the self that results from role-playing. To cast one's self in a role or to live within the confines of an assigned role is, in effect, to live like a thing. The self is encased in an opaque and object-like exterior which conducts life on the self's behalf. Actually the role one plays is a displacement of the self, a robot-like alternative to human existence as a person. One may recall Headstone's self-repressed, de-personalized existence as Schoolteacher, a term which Eugene Wrayburn scornfully uses for him in place of his name. Thus Bumble, who had originally cast Oliver in the role of "parish boy," casts himself in the equally de-personalized role of "beadle," of which, ironically, he is very proud.

Plainly enough, then, role-playing is "philosophical" in the novel's sense. In the course of playing roles, we make use of our malleability, which is the malleability of man as a lump of matter, and deny or suppress the rest. To gain our object through role-playing, we must "de-selve," and Dickens draws our attention to the greatness of this cost in the satire on Bumble the Beadle. Meanwhile, Fagin's self-assigned role is that of an honest if rather miserly member of the commercial class. In what he likes to call his "trade," "profession," or "business," he maintains a functional pretense with which those under him are made to play along. Here great stress is laid on the usefulness of their roles to Fagin and his associates. And so attractive as well as efficacious are they in their roles that some doubt is raised whether the self-distortion and self-loss of role-playing so evident in the case of Bumble is a feature of the lower world at all. Furthermore, as in Nancy's case, characters must play roles in order to do good as well as to do evil. However, the main force of the novel in this connection goes to showing up the perils of role-playing. Above all, it convincingly demonstrates the vulnerability of role-playing to sentimentalism, which is, we come to see, the locus of a resistance to any fallaciously reductive or mechanistic version of the self. The sentimental is the orientation to the discovery of the real self, and so finds expression in a distrust of surfaces. As role-players, we are vulnerable to those who, by virtue of their instinctive attention to inner truths, are not fooled by the substitution of the role for the self, who see through it, and withhold ultimate credence. Herein lies the vulnerability of Fagin and his gang to the sentimental hero of the novel, Nancy.

To Oliver, too, the thieves are vulnerable. "He has been the—the—somehow the cause of all this," says Fagin in his cell (lii). And there is enormous irony in this plaintive confession from the seemingly indomitable villain that he has been undone by the most innocent of children, even by the standards of Victorian fiction. But the vulnerability of Fagin to Oliver lies in Oliver's mysterious intractability. He cannot be molded into a thief, as Monks too observes:

"I saw it was not easy to train him to the business," replied the Jew; "he was not like other boys in the same circumstances."
"Curse him, no!" muttered the man, "or he would have been a thief long ago."   (xxvi, 170)

The reason that Oliver is "not like other boys" is probably the one given in Chapter Two, that "nature or inheritance had implanted a good sturdy spirit in Oliver's breast." Needless to say, this is not terribly convincing. Only in the assault on Noah does Oliver seem aware himself of any such resource. But the very word "spirit" bears significantly upon the failure of Monks's and Fagin's scheme. "Philosophically," they reckon without "considerations of heart," and so the effort to convert the boy to thievery comes to nothing.

The vulnerability of the thieves to Nancy, however, takes a broader form and has a broader and more passionate significance. In what is easily one of the finest scenes of the novel, when Oliver has been returned to the den and is being beaten by Fagin, Nancy steps in to prevent his murder:

> "What do you mean by this?" said Sikes; backing the inquiry with a very common imprecation concerning the most beautiful of human features . . . "what do you mean by it? Burn my body! Do you know who you are, and what you are?"
>
> "Oh, yes, I know all about it," replied the girl, laughing hysterically; and shaking her head from side to side, with a poor assumption of indifference.
>
> "Well, then, keep quiet," rejoined Sikes, with a growl like that he was accustomed to use when addressing his dog, "or I'll quiet you for a good long time to come."
>
> The girl laughed again: even less composedly than before; and, darting a hasty look at Sikes, turned her face aside, and bit her lip till the blood came.
>
> "You're a nice one," added Sikes, as he surveyed her with a contemptuous air, "to take up the humane and gen—teel side! A pretty subject for the child, as you call him, to make a friend of!"

"God Almighty help me, I am!" cried the girl
passionately; "and I wish I had been struck dead in the street,
or had changed places with them we passed so near to-night,
before I had lent a hand in bringing him here. He's a thief, a
liar, a devil, all that's bad, from this night forth. Isn't that
enough for the old wretch without blows?"

"Come, come, Sikes," said the Jew, appealing to him in a
remonstratory tone, and motioning towards the boys, who
were eagerly attentive to all that passed; "we must have civil
words; civil words, Bill."

"Civil words!" cried the girl, whose passion was frightful
to see. "Civil words, you villain! Yes, you deserve 'em from
me. I thieved for you when I was a child not half as old as
this!" pointing to Oliver. "I have been in the same trade, and
in the same service, for twelve years since. Don't you know it?
Speak out! don't you know it?"

"Well, well," replied the Jew, with an attempt at
pacification; "and if you have, it's your living!"

"Aye, it is!" returned the girl; not speaking, but pouring
out the words in one continuous and vehement scream. "It is
my living; and the cold, wet, dirty streets are my home; and
you're the wretch that drove me to them long ago; and that'll
keep me there, day and night, day and night, till I die!"

"I shall do you a mischief!" interposed the Jew, goaded
by these reproaches; "a mischief worse than that, if you say
much more!"   (xvi, 103–4)

There is central significance in Sikes's quaint reference to
Oliver as "the child, as you call him." Nancy is she who
calls a child a child, a thief a thief, a wretch a wretch. She
is terrifying, "pouring out the words in one continuous
and vehement scream," precisely because of her lack of
pretense, because she *does* know who she is and what
she is. She frankly admits that she is not a fit model to
the boy, thus dissociating herself from Fagin's pretension
of keeping school. She ridicules the euphemism that her

prostitution is a "living." She will not have any part of the middle-class affectation, including the affectation of decency: "Civil words!" She rejects the pretense of hearth and home that is kept up in the den. She rejects the utility of role-playing, and its pragmatic justification, preferring instead direct moral judgments: "a thief, a liar, a devil, all that's bad." She is able to see through everything, and appropriately it is her eyes that are damned by Sikes.

He will, we remember, have greater cause to damn them later. When, near the end, he dies, apparently by an accident he has caused himself, it is the case upon closer inspection that he has been actively pursued to his death by a real and potent adversary:

> At that very instant the murderer, looking behind him on the roof, threw his arms above his head, and uttered a yell of terror.
> "The eyes again!" he cried in an unearthly screech.
> Staggering as if struck by lightning, he lost his balance and tumbled over the parapet.   (I, 347)

The eyes of Nancy are an active force. Just as they pierce the self-defensive structures of role-playing and mutual reification in Fagin's den, they force upon Sikes a recognition of the guilt from which he would flee. In the murder scene, he prevents Nancy from drawing the curtain to let in light—"There's light enough for wot I've got to do"—and is described after the deed is done as "shutting out the sight with his hands" (xlvii, 322). But Nancy embodies, even in death, the urgent imperative to drag the truth into the light—in the words of the preface to the Third Edition, to see things "as they really are" (p. lxii).

Among several ironies here, it is most important to

note that, from the first, Sikes himself has been portrayed as a kind of realist. Like Nancy and unlike Fagin, he rejects the false self of role-playing, and rejects affectation generally. "Speak out and call things by their right names," he exclaims at one point (xix, 122). When Fagin concludes an oath, "upon my honor," Sikes is quick to respond contemptuously, "Upon your *what?*" (xxxix, 260). If Fagin is a "philosophical" charater in the novel's special use of the term, Bill Sikes has a "philosphical" attribute on more ordinary grounds. He would not obfuscate, he would define his terms. But how is this willingness to look the truth in the eye to be reconciled to his flight from Nancy's eyes and the truth they habitually saw? And there is a matching and opposite contradiction in Nancy, not at first apparent—a mixture, as it were, of "hard" and "soft" elements. If she is a more unflinching realist than Sikes, on the one hand, she is also, on the other, joined to the positively ethereal Rose Maylie by a bond of "original nature." Like Rose, she is soft on Oliver. Her realism seems here to be a property of her sentimentalism, aligned with the latter against the "philosophical" pretense of a Fagin, or such avoidance of truth as Sikes's. It is sentimental, precisely, to perceive rightly that "philosophy," as Dickens means it, is self-deceiving, an evasion and a mask.

As with realism, so it is with pragmatism of outlook, another ordinarily "philosophical" attribute. When Nancy promises, in a burst of romantic feeling, that she will walk around the prison all night if he should ever be inside waiting to be hanged, the "unsentimental Mr. Sikes" inquires "what good that would do" (xvi, 99). He objects to Nancy's "woman's nonsense" because it does not work. But in fact Nancy is extraordinarily successful in her plans, and it is Sikes, ultimately, who fails.

Her power to act, in the double sense, like her powers to see and to expose, derives precisely from the fact that she is not "philosophical" but "sentimental." Fagin tries, at one point, to play on Nancy's sentimental susceptibilities for his own ends:

> "Poor leetle child! Left in a ditch, Nance; only think!"
> "The child," said the girl, suddenly looking up, "is better where he is, than among us. . . . I shall be glad to have him away from my eyes, and to know that the worst is over. I can't bear to have him about me. The sight of him turns me against myself, and all of you." (xxvi, 166)

Although Nancy is faking to deceive Fagin, she tells the truth. The sight of Oliver, the feelings he evokes in her, will turn her against herself and against those upon whom she depends for well-being. The plot as a whole, and the destiny of every character, will hinge on this self-revulsion in Nancy, which runs, we may note, exactly contrary to Fagin's elaborate theory of self-interest. Nancy moves the novel's world, not because it is an inane world in which she alone is clever, but because it is an unfeeling and unseeing world in which she alone sees and is moved. Her feelings are not a source of weakness but of efficacy; her sentimentalism is not passive virtue but active strength.

That Nancy is the hero proper—not, with its other connotations, the heroine—of *Oliver Twist* is not often observed. It is usual to say that Oliver is the hero, meaning that he is the central character, and it is sometimes held that his passivity, rather than being an objection to his heroism, is actually his pedigree as a hero of Dickens' special kind. For Dickens, the argument goes, was inclined to see action as tainted, and, as a result, his heroes are generally passive.[10] There is strong evidence for this view in the weakness of Oliver, but it should be modified by an awareness of Dickens' self-conscious variations on the standard equation of hero to central character. *David Copperfield* famously begins with a somewhat teasing dubiety on this point: "Whether I shall turn out to be the hero of my own life, or whether that station will be held by anybody else, these pages must show." Oliver stands as firmly at the center of his novel as does David or Pip, and yet Pip occupies, comparatively, a good deal more of thematic terrain of his novel than the others do of theirs. And Pip shares the *topoi* of heroism not with Oliver but with Nancy: the change of heart, the self-discovery through self-sacrifice, the return to "original nature." It may be objected that Magwitch is the nearer equivalent to Nancy, because his plot-making generosity to the central character resembles Nancy's sacrifice for Oliver. And yet Magwitch's generosity is only summarized retrospectively at the end, not experienced, like Nancy's, as, indeed, the central action of the novel.

3

The power of the sentimental Nancy—to see, to feel, to act—figures so prominently in *Oliver Twist* largely because of the kind of novel that at least on one level it is intended to be: a novel of social evils. The reformer-journalist, it seems, when first he turns his hand to novels, retains the decidedly affective inclinations of that trade.[11] In such writing, the reader is the object of a design which the writer makes no attempt to conceal. It is divisible into three stages. First, the reader must be made to see what he ordinarily does not see, or avoids seeing. Then his presumed insensitivity to what he sees must be worn away. Finally, he must be made to feel what the author deems he ought to feel about what he has been shown. How the sight of Oliver affects Nancy may be taken as a metaphor for how the exposure of public scandal is meant to work upon the novel-reading public.

The Preface to the Third Edition argues boastfully that the author's second novel performed "a service to society" in showing the denizens of the underworld "as they really are." The same would apply, presumably, to the novel's depiction of the Poor Law abuses. Thus the over-arching defense is a simple avowal of realism: "IT IS TRUE."

But there are people of so refined and delicate a nature, that they cannot bear the contemplation of such horrors. Not that they turn instinctively from crime; but that criminal characters, to suit them, must be, like their meat, in delicate disguise . . . Now, as the stern and plain truth . . . was a part of the purpose of this book, I will not, for these readers, abate one hole in the Dodger's coat, or one scrap of curl-paper in the girl's dishevelled hair.   (p. lxiii)

On the contrary, of course, it became Dickens' habit to add holes and scraps of curl-paper in order to arrest our attention by the outrage of our feelings. He is then in a position to explode our "romantic" illusions about "such horrors" and force us to see what is "really there." Just so, at the death of Jo in *Bleak House,* a later Dickens will remind his readers with context-wrenching abruptness, that *real* children are "dying thus around us, every day."

It is a truth he would force us, through his fiction, to see and feel.

The novel strategically presumes, that is, a "philosophical" audience, perpetrating a "philosophical" avoidance of the truth, and inured against the moral reproach inherent in what it sees—like Fagin, gazing composedly on the sleeping Oliver with a clear conscience, unmoved against himself (xix). Much is made, in the novel, of the culpability not only of "out-and-outers" like Fagin, but of the by-standing middle class. Fagin's commercial bourgeois pretense redounds to the discredit of that sector no less than to his own. A case in point, especially relevant to the guilty insensibility of the audience Dickens addresses, is Sowerberry, the undertaker. He is ironically, comically praised for his ability to witness scenes of horror without being markedly affected. This is the Dickens, one is reminded, of which Evelyn Waugh was so fond. "Well, Oliver," says Sowerberry, after having seen to the burial of a poor woman with the most casual brutality, "how do you like it?"

"Pretty well, thank you, sir," replied Oliver, with considerable hesitation. "Not very much, sir."

"Ah, you'll get used to it in time, Oliver," said Sowerberry. "Nothing to it when you *are* used to it, my boy."

Oliver wondered, in his own mind, whether it had taken a very long time to get Mr. Sowerberry used to it. (v, 34)

The implication is that there is a class of men, not Fagins but men in respectable professions, to whom such insensitivity comes easily, nevertheless.

No doubt there is an earnest and a convinced (if also a simple) moralism in what this suggests about Dickens' purposes as a novelist. Perhaps it is his seeming assumption that a moral judgment inheres in what we see, as if moral qualities were visible, like colors, that, more than anything else, distances him from the regnant modern sensibility. But his moral vision was not really so naive. What was distinctive about it was that, for reasons that should be clear by now, he valued moral instinct over moral reasoning. In setting up his reader as Sowerberry, he did not intend a simple accusation of insensitivity. He was aware, for example, that the reader would no doubt have observed the harmful effects on others of his own irresponsibility or malfeasance with compunctions and remorse. But even such apparently immediate responses, as Dickens understood, actually occur at the end of a calculation based upon learned and finally arbitrary cultural and ethical arrangements of responsibility, and it was to his purpose to assail such arrangements as "philosophical." They proceed from "maxim and theory," and, although not "putting entirely out of sight any considerations of heart, or generous impulse and feeling," they organize such considerations so as to maximize benefits mutually and to amortize pains—as Hobbes explained long before, and as Fagin explains to Noah Claypole.

It is significant that Dickens places this logic in the mouth of his villain. Only rarely does any Dickens novel seem to quarrel with the societal arrangement as a whole. Instead, his method generally is to display innocence of an awareness of the necessity for such arrangements, and so strip society of its protective rationalizations. His aim is to refresh and enliven our response to the actuality of sordidness and suffering by depriving us of the comfort of supersubtle explanations for their necessity and "utility." For Dickens' purposes, the Utilitarian calculus of the "greater good" can be described, in the language of an earlier chapter, as a way of linguistically assimilating into a societal whole with an appearance of harmony and integrity what are in reality rank injustices and contradictions in the public weal. It is on the unbudging reality of injustice that Dickens takes his stand: "IT IS TRUE." Again, the writer's allegiance to the real is nearly allied to his distrust of system.

Thus Dickens' treatment of moral attributes as if they were visible or material is ultimately a figurative strategy, a useful manner of speaking, rather than evidence of a moral simplism. He seeks to create in us an undiluted, impulsive response to social wrongs. He wants us to see them in such a way that we see that they are wrongs.[12] So it is that Nancy's eyes can function in *Oliver Twist* as an active moral force. For Dickens, moral feeling is not so much an effect of perception as a means. The sentimentalist perceives truths to which the philosopher is blind.

5. The Novel of Reality:
Dombey and Son

"What I want, is frankness, confidence, less conventionality,
and freer play of soul. We are so dreadfully artificial."
— Mrs. Skewton (xxi, 284)

"We are dreadfully real, Mr. Carker . . . are we not?"
— Mrs. Skewton (xxvii, 373)

No doubt it was prudent of John Forster to dissuade
Dickens from affixing to *Martin Chuzzlewit* the epigraph
he had intended for it: "Your homes the scene, yourselves the actors, here!"[1] Dickens' great friend and biographer does not deny that the motto expresses rather well
a central purpose of the novel, which has for its villain
not a thug like Sikes nor a gangster like Quilp, but Pecksniff, respected architect and family man, who is devoted
with apparently effective self-deception to Truth and to
Virtue, and who is shown in an early plate seated com-
fortably before the hearth flanked by Mercy and Charity,
his daughters. The intended motto suggests that Dickens
imagines the main portion of his readership similarly

seated and flanked, and now means to turn upon them his keen critical eyes, lately busy seeing America. Presumably Forster felt that Dickens' hearthside preeminence was too great an asset to be risked. It is interesting to note that Dickens, uncounselled, would have risked it so openly, especially because it is so popular (and smug) an observation among Dickens' latter-day readers that he adjusted his designs to please the contemporary audience.

Indeed, even without the epigraph, the application of the story of Pecksniff was not missed, and the novel, if only partly for that reason, was Dickens' least popular in his lifetime.[2] Moreover, commencing with the creation of Pecksniff, Dickens was to be relentless in identifying deceit, hypocrisy, and greed in British society's most respectable, "responsible," and *ordinary* personages and institutions: Dombeys, Merdles, Tulkinghorns. Bernard Shaw admirably paraphrased what was increasingly Dickens' drift in this period, the novels of which he took to be saying "that it is not our disorder but our order that is horrible."[3]

In that development of Dickens as social critic that the mention of *Martin Chuzzlewit* (1844), *Bleak House* (1853), and *Little Dorrit* (1857) suggests, *Dombey and Son* (1848) occupies a position of special interest. The study of Dombey is domestic and intimate, like the study of Pecksniff, but more intense and thorough. He is seen largely through the eyes of near relations—daughter, son, wife, sister—but also, to give the fullest possible perspective on a yet inscrutable man, he is seen through the eyes of persons at widely different degrees of distance from him—Carker's, Toodle's, the "Game Chicken's." The em-

anation of Dombey's personal power at all levels dominates this novel as Pecksniff dominates *Chuzzlewit*. But
also Dombey, or the firm which bears his name, dominates the novel for most of its length as Chancery and the
Circumlocution Office dominate theirs. That is, he com-
pounds the personal, psychological evil of the earlier
novel with the larger, impersonal, apparently arbitrary
evil of the later. Thus we have in Dombey an individual
who represents within himself his society's own concat-
enation of ills, private and public, local and far-reaching,
knowable and obscure. He is ultimately an epitome of
the society, and it is altogether to the point that his tem-
perament seems at times to be stereotypically "mid-
Victorian" and Anglo-Saxon. For *Dombey and Son,* of all
Dickens' novels, is the one most directly and abundantly
concerned with the quotidian Victorian realities, the
transcendently usual in the life of his time and place, and
also of his class. "Your homes the scene, yourselves the
actors, here!": The epigraph would not entirely be appropriate for this novel, because Dombey is rich and his
home in that respect extraordinary. But from another
point of view the words fall short of expressing how in-
tently Dickens has focused upon the life of the middle
class in *Dombey*. For if its central character is the exact
type of a few, he is nonetheless the end case and logical
consummation of the many. Dombey is not an aristocrat
by blood. He is a "successful" businessman, as that word
continues to be used, raised above his social station a
generation or two ago by the acquisition of money. The
implicit standards against which his home life is judged
are—sometimes notoriously—middle-class standards.
Not "yourselves" as you are, then, but yourselves as it is

your deepest tendency and even aspiration to become, your ideal and quintessential selves, are the heroes, here.

In short, *Dombey and Son* is Dickens' great novel of the bourgeoisie at home. An indirect but, as I imagine, rewarding approach to the novel in this one of its aspects lies through a document that is of great interest in its own right: Thomas Mann's "Homage" to Franz Kafka (1940).[4] The occasion of the "Homage" was the publication of a new edition of *The Castle,* a novel in which the middle-class home is a house of unpredictable horrors, its people dim, unreal, or grotesque. Mann's paradoxical interpretation, in essence, is that Kafka was a "dreamer" who dreamed not of mystical perfections but of "the blisses of the commonplace"—a phrase from Mann's own *Tonio Kröger.* K.'s attempted relations with the bourgeois community around the castle all founder in a drama of incomprehensibility. But in K.'s agony of isolation Mann detects an aspiration akin to the artist Kröger's "longing for simple human feeling" and "love of the blond and good and ordinary."[5]

To the already unlikely company of himself and Kafka, Mann's essay admits a third: Gustave Flaubert. The significant anecdote he tells of Flaubert's later years begins with a description of the novelist that is itself a significant exaggeration:

The famous aesthete, who in an ascetic paroxysm sacrificed all his life to his nihilistic idol, *"littérature,"* once paid a visit with his niece, Mme Commanville, to a family of her acquaintance, a sturdy and happy wedded pair surrounded by a flock of charming children. On the way home the author of the *Tentation de Saint Antoine* was very thoughtful. Walking with Mme Commanville along the Seine, he kept coming back to the natural, healthy, jolly, upright life he had just had a glimpse of. *"Ils sont dans le vrai!"* he kept repeating.[6]

D'être dans le vrai Mann translates as "to live in the true and the right." There is reason to share with Mann his sense of the irony of Flaubert's words, when we recall that the world Flaubert here apostrophizes for the surpassing trueness of its existence is the same which in an earlier mood he immortally savaged as *le Bovarisme.* And the irony is compounded when Mann reports that "this phrase, this complete abandonment of his whole position, from the lips of the master whose creed had been the denial of life for the sake of art—this phase had been Kafka's favorite quotation."

The attitudinal parallels that emerge in Mann's shrewd essay among these great, diverse geniuses of the novel illustrate the complex and self-troubled history of the genre's relation to the middle class, a history of tangled admiration and contempt for the class which is usually given credit for the origins of the novel and which constituted, for a hundred years, almost its only audience. In the conventional chronology of the matter, it is with Flaubert that the novel becomes for the first time conscious of itself as a "fine art"—it had been conscious of itself as fiction from the beginning—and expresses its new aestheticism partly through a painstakingness of method and partly through a rebellious flurry of disdain for the novel-reading class, on whose behalf, arguably, Emma Bovary suffers considerable humiliations. But what Mann's anecdote supplies puts in doubt the sincerity of Flaubert's disdain. We profit from the hint that Flaubert the aesthete secretly envies the butchers and druggists of the provinces for the very blandness of their daily existence. Perhaps, just as the distance Charles Bovary involuntarily puts between himself and Emma preserves his gross illusions about her, so the distance of irony that Flaubert interposes between himself and Bovary serves in fact to keep intact, until late in his life, a naive conviction of the superior claims of the bourgeois life to reality and authenticity of being.

I have suggested that in *Dombey and Son* Dickens' vision of ordinary middle-class life finds its most thorough and palpable expression.[7] Many readers agree, I think, that it is his least drastic creation, his least fantastic, and perhaps also his least "picturesque." Many react negatively to the peculiar sobriety and greyness of its tone. But in fact what shows in the execution of this novel cannot truly be called restraint. Dickens' energies are engaged in it as powerfully as ever, and as a result it is among his extreme successes of dramatic or melodramatic writing. But they are engaged in the representation of a nearer reality than, say, the persecutions of Nell— engaged with realities more known and therefore less tractable, paradoxically more puzzling. Dickens never exiled himself from the middle class. What he famously suffered in youth was not apostasy from family life but a forced separation, which for him could not end too soon. He willed himself into a marriage and a family very early, and lived a family life even after the separation from Kate. And because he was not an exile, he had none of the exile's nostalgia such as Mann detects in Flaubert, Kafka, and himself, or such as we cannot fail to detect in Proust or Joyce: none of the looking back with longing for what they imagine as the wholesomeness and truth of the life left behind. Instead, Dickens' vision in *Dombey* is located emphatically *amid* bourgeois normalcy and domesticity, among nurses and governesses, baptisms and weddings, storekeepers, messenger boys, and office lackeys. Let us see if it is his judgment that life under the aegis of Dombeyism is lived *dans le vrai.*

2

How self-consciously and even profoundly "domestic" a novel is *Dombey and Son* can best be seen in the great importance it attaches to the domestic arrangements of its characters.[8] The dwellings of a large number of major and minor characters are presented in detail and as an intrinsic part of their characterization. We have seen something of this in a previous chapter, where a description of Dombey in his study was closely considered, although much more could be said not only of that description but also of the topographical characterization of Dombey that appears in the rest of his house as well as in the offices of the firm. Of course, from Bob Sawyer's chambers in *Pickwick* to Boffin's Bower in *Our Mutual Friend*, Dickens always made use of the suggestivity of environment for character, and the difference in *Dombey* is first of all one of quantity. The Wooden Midshipman's house, Cuttle's quarters in Brig Place, Mrs. Pipchin's castle, the Blimbers' establishment exhaustively, Toots's sporting apartment, Miss Tox's, the Toodles' in Staggs's Gardens, and the very different residences of Carker the Manager and Carker Junior comprise a partial list. This very proliferation carries perhaps a suggestion of its own, and it may be that the idea of domicile in *Dombey* has a special purpose, which a look at the presentation of a less prominent abode than Dombey's perhaps will clarify.

In Chapter Seven, entitled "A Bird's-eye Glimpse of Miss Tox's Dwelling-Place; also of the State of Miss Tox's Affections," the interior of her house is described only after its situation in Princess' Place has been thoroughly rendered:

> Miss Tox inhabited a dark little house that had been squeezed, at some remote period of English History, into a fashionable neighbourhood at the west end of town, where it stood in the shade like a poor relation of the great street round the corner, coldly looked down upon by mighty mansions. It was not exactly in a court, and it was not exactly in a yard; but it was in the dullest of No-Thoroughfares, rendered anxious and haggard by distant double knocks.   (vii, 85)

Not only is the house placed in the street, but the street is placed in relation to other streets, and "placed" not only geographically, but with reference to a hierarchy of prestige. The latter is by no means a matter of indifference to Miss Tox:

> Perhaps, taken altogether, from top to bottom, it was the most inconvenient little house in England, and the crookedest; but then, Miss Tox said, what a situation! There was very little daylight to be got there in the winter: no sun at the best of times: air was out of the question, and traffic was walled out. Still Miss Tox said, think of the situation!   (vii, 86)

"Situation" is one of a group of related terms in the novel that play an important thematic role. For one thing, characters are continually reminded that they must know their place, station, or position, knowledge of which is Miss Tox's special province:

"Louisa," said Mr. Dombey, one day, to his sister, "I really think I must present your friend Miss Tox with some little token, on the occasion of Paul's christening. She has exerted herself so warmly in the child's behalf from the first, and seems to understand her position so thoroughly (a very rare merit in this world, I am sorry to say), that it would really be agreeable to me to notice her."

Let it be no detraction from the merits of Miss Tox, to hint that in Mr. Dombey's eyes, as in some others that occasionally see the light, they only achieved that mighty piece of knowledge, the understanding of their own position, who showed a fitting reverence for his.   (v, 47)

The novel's distinctive pairing of persons from different extremes of economic status—Toodle and Dombey, for instance, or the Carker Brothers, or Edith and Alice—is another way of calling attention to the matter of their relative "positions." In another sense of the word, the scientific instruments of Sol Gills's shop have for their purpose the exact designation of position, although they are of no avail in the painful guessing as to the situation of the "Son and Heir" on which Walter has sailed. And the whole question of position is given a curious twist by an ingenious speculation of Captain Cuttle's, powerful enough to stop him short in his admiration of Gills:

"But he's chockfull of science," he observed, waving his hook toward the stock-in-trade. "Look ye here! Here's a collection of 'em. Earth, air, or water. It's all one . . .

"Ah!" he said, with a sigh, "it's a fine thing to understand 'em. And yet it's a fine thing not to understand 'em. I hardly know which is best. It's so comfortable to sit here and feel that you might be weighed, measured, magnified, electrified, polarized, played the very devil with: and never know how."   (iv, 45)

Here Cuttle speaks up for the pleasures of being firmly "situated," even of being situated in some unknowable scheme by unknowable means. In the literature of the century which is called Romantic, such a hymn to dependency and to ignorant security is a rarity. And a recollection of Cuttle's sentiment returns, heavy with irony, later in the novel, where the Captain's putative enjoyment of being "played the very devil with" is severely tested by Carker. Carker manipulates Cuttle and Walter Gay by means of an exact calculation, on his part, of their "positions."

When we do reach the interior of Miss Tox's house, we find its contents "situated" in terms of another variable, time:

> The dingy tenement inhabited by Miss Tox was her own;
> having been devised and bequeathed to her by the deceased
> owner of the fishy eye in the locket, of whom a miniature
> portrait, with a powdered head and a pigtail, balanced the
> kettle holder on opposite sides of the parlour fireplace. The
> greater part of the furniture was of the powdered-head and
> pig-tail period; comprising a plate-warmer, always languishing
> and sprawling its four attenuated bow legs in somebody's
> way; and an obsolete harpsichord, illuminated round the
> maker's name with a painted garland of sweet peas.   (vii, 86)

Consistent with the idea of *Dealings with the Firm of Dombey and Son*, financial information about the house is conscientiously imparted at the beginning of the description: Miss Tox owns her house outright, whereas Major Bagstock's, across the way, is "let Furnished" to him by a "retired butler who had married a housekeeper." The temporal "fix" that is established on Miss Tox's, meanwhile, is double in form. The furniture is associated with a more or less precise historical period. It is Georgian, an epoch of the near past to which Dickens attached considerable importance in his personal mythology.[9] Secondly, Miss Tox's possession of the apartment is fixed in an implied genealogical succession. She inherited the house from her father, whose visual image is present within it. As so often in the novel, the present is rendered by comparison to an image of the past, the living by comparison to the dead.

When the "deceased owner of the fishy eye in the locket" is first mentioned, in the initial appearance of Miss Tox in Chapter One, it is added that the eye had "no approach to speculation in it." Banquo is invoked, it may be, to call attention to the fact that a company of significant ghosts stands behind the novel as one stands behind *Macbeth*.[10] Of course, the first Mrs. Dombey and, later, Paul are the most prominent examples. But Edith, too, has lost a son and a husband, "Granger of Ours," (xxi), as well as a father whose brother, Alice's father, is also dead. Countless minor ghosts like the elder Tox are projected: Pipchin of the Peruvian Mines, the mother of the happy family of daughters across the street from Dombey's, a (quite redundant) Toodle "babby," and even an elder brother for Bagstock (x). Their purpose collectively is to further "situate" the characters of the present generation. Readings of *Dombey* generally take account of the important function of time and change in the novel, and the symbolic function of their consummation, death.[11] But here it is useful especially to note that time is also a coordinate, paired with space, that participates in a general activity of locating or fixing individuals. Individuals are, in Cuttle's words, "weighed, mea-

sured, magnified, electrified, polarized," for the purpose
of establishing a definitive locus for each. And it is this
defining fixedness of which the idea of domicile is perhaps chiefly expressive.

The importance of the idea of domicile, however, is
clearest when characters are separated from their
homes—as they are, most often by force, repeatedly
throughout the novel. Such separation, moreover, is
always experienced as a catastrophe. Cuttle is exiled from
Brig Place, Gay is sent off and Gills follows; Florence is,
at one point, lost, and much later she must flee; Edith
and Carker flee; Paul travels, metaphorically, from a temporary home to a permanent, "true" one. He is said to
have lived "as if he had taken life unfurnished, and the
upholsterer were never coming" (xi, 149). Furthermore,
homes themselves alter, and these alterations, too, have a
mostly negative significance. The somber alterations in
the Dombey house after the death of the first Mrs. Dombey are reversed grandly after the second marriage (xx-
viii: "Alterations") and reversed again when the furniture and the house are sold (xxxix). The changes in
Staggs's Gardens, uprooted by the railway, are, for different reasons, of equal moment. The disturbing implications of domestic alteration in the novel seem to suggest
themselves to Walter Gay as he looks around in his bed-
room for the last time before departing on the "Son and
Heir":

Dismantled of his little stock of books and pictures, it looked
coldly and reproachfully on him for his desertion, and had
already a foreshadowing upon it of its coming strangeness. "A
few hours more," thought Walter, "and no dream I ever had
here when I was a school-boy will be so little mine as this old

room. The dream may come back in my sleep, and I may
return waking to this place, it may be: but the dream at least
will serve no other master, and the room may have a score,
and every one of them may change, neglect, misuse it.''
(xix, 254)

Walter's misgivings reflect a sense that one's "place" and
one's vulnerabilities are nearly related. Awareness of unwelcome "change," of "neglect, misuse" in Florence's life
and his own no doubt inform these musings. Moreover,
one is vulnerable through one's past connections to
"place," because place is external, physical, and may be
altered, whereas dreams of the past, though remote, are
yet internal and therefore secure.

   Miss Tox's apartments are not themselves free from
change, as the Major across the way, with whom she has
been conducting a "Platonic" flirtation, sees through his
spy-glass:

She had been wont, once upon a time, to look out at one of
her little dark windows by accident, and blushingly return the
Major's greeting; but now, she never gave the Major a chance,
and cared nothing at all whether he looked over the way or
not. Other changes had come to pass too. The Major, standing
in the shade of his own apartment, could make out that an air
of greater smartness had recently come over Miss Tox's
house.   (vii, 88)

The list of changes which follows is less telling for our
purposes than this glimpse of Major Bagstock, "standing
in the shade of his own apartment," or the implied picture of former times, when the Major and Miss Tox spied
each other from opposite sides of Princess' Place, out of
the dark or shaded windows of their separate dwellings.
On consideration, these images confirm and further what

Walter's idea of the vulnerability of the self embodied in one's dwelling-place has already suggested, that the home is, for Dickens, not an "extension" of the self, which is the figure usually assigned to it in discussions of "realistic" setting, but rather just the opposite of an "extension." It is an emblem of one's limitations, expressive of the inexorably limited purview, the inexorably *given* sphere of existence, that is alloted to each of us. "Situated" just as it is in space and time, the home defines the limits both of one's vision of the world and of the extent to which one can oneself be seen and known. It matters very much, therefore, that the novel is peopled to such a large extent with characters shut up within the confines of their domestic settings, spying each other out of windows—bound to their distinctive and defining points of survey.

When the actual changes in Miss Tox's house are consulted, we find that

a new bird cage had been provided for the ancient little canary bird; that divers ornaments, cut out of coloured card-boards and paper, seemed to decorate the chimney-piece and tables; that a plant or two had suddenly sprung up in the windows; that Miss Tox occasionally practised on the harpsichord, whose garland of sweet peas was now always displayed ostentatiously, crowned with the Copenhagen and Bird Waltzes in a Music Book of Miss Tox's own copying. (vii, 88)

Such marvellous specificity and rightness have to do with Dickens' asseveration, in the "Preface" of 1867, that "I know, in my fancy, every stair in the little midshipman's house, and could swear to every pew in the church in which Florence was married, or to every young gentle-

man's bedstead in Doctor Blimber's establishment"
(p. 834). In *Dombey*, I have already said, Dickens turns
his eye upon near, familiar realities. But the issue here is
not one of verisimilitude. We are struck, instead, by
what is better described as thoroughness of imaginary
knowledge. The novel contains a number of descriptions
equal or greater in such thoroughness, and, when this is
noted, it is not unlikely that Balzac will come to mind. Is
this not the thoroughness Balzac displays in describing
the Maison Vauquer, or, to choose an example from a
book whose similarities to *Dombey* are striking in several
respects, Old Grandet's house in Saumur? Is this different, in short, from the descriptive genius of main-
stream realism, in which the doorjamb, the flowers in the
window, and the expression in the eye are all recorded
with the same "objectivity" and exactitude of impression?

   To answer, the above citation from the "Preface"
must be restored to its full context:

   I began this book by the Lake of Geneva, and went on
   with it for some months in France, before pursuing it in
   England. The association between the writing and the place of
   writing is so curiously strong in my mind, that at this day,
   although I know, in my fancy, every stair in the little
   midshipman's house, and could swear to every pew in the
   church in which Florence was married, or to every young
   gentleman's bedstead in Doctor Blimber's establishment, I yet
   confusedly imagine Captain Cuttle as secluding himself from
   Mrs. MacStinger among the mountains of Switzerland.
   Similarly, when I am reminded by any chance of what it was
   that the waves were always saying, my remembrance wanders
   for a whole winter night about the streets of Paris—as I

restlessly did with a heavy heart, on the night when I had
written the chapter in which my little friend and I parted
company.   (p. 834, with emendations of 1867 according to
note.)

Dickens' retrospective confusion contains a valuable clue
to the activity of his visual imagination within the novel.
Stretching between the precisely known, painstakingly
realized individual domestic and institutional interiors,
there is a spottiness of topography, a placelessness, a lack
of focus. It is a landscape full of holes. The treacherous
unreality of what lies between one home and another is
illustrated at several points. Cuttle cannot set foot outside
Brig Place without danger, nor return to it once he has
left. Alice's wanderings are her disgrace. The horrors of
being lost, of flight and escape, have already been mentioned. Dombey's train journey to Brighton after Paul's
death, and Carker's return to England make the general
point clearer. There is hardly such a thing as a pleasant
journey in the novel, except Paul's last.

One way of describing the impression that results is
to say that it is as if, when the local, near details are
brought into focus, the interconnections between loci
blur and disappear. One has abundance of detail, but
only at the expense of wholeness. Thus there is again the
proliferation of "worlds," of points of view and spheres
of experience, such as was noted in the introduction of
six "worlds" in seven chapters at the beginning of *Our
Mutual Friend*. The effect is alternately one of fragmen-
tariness and of a competition of pretended wholenesses,
necessarily incommensurate and exclusive of one another, and each deficient in some way that the novel in
the course of events reveals.

Balzac's vast sociological intent in the *Comédie* is surely too complex and sophisticated, too bound up with purposes other than sociological, to be put aside as a "pretended wholeness," but just as surely his plan is in its own way an apotheosis of totalization. Individual, detailed descriptions in Balzac's novels are in fact meticulously stitched together, within each novel and from one novel to another. It is the life of France over several decades that is stitched together, urban to provincial, military to religious, and so on. After all, Balzac's master plan is recognizably a strategy for living with that awareness of formal limitation in the novel which, as I have said, weighs so heavily on the realist's mind. Balzac seems to say that, if novels, no matter how realistic, necessarily draw fictive limits at their borders, perhaps one can join together several, many, a quasi-infinite number of novels at their borders, and so make up a sufficiently expansive quilt, as it were, of representation.

In his evident method in *Dombey*, Dickens forswears such stitching together, and denies to all of his characters, and also to himself and to the reader, the benefit of any comprehensive overview of the kind Balzac intends. In fact Dickens is under no less severe a representational compulsion than Balzac, but his strategy for coping with the novel's representational limits—and it is no less a strategy than Balzac's—is quite different. It is, as we have seen before, to confess, by the very multitude of rival perspectives on reality in the novel, the final insufficiency and arbitrariness of any one perspective, even the novel's own. However, as its negative ring should tell us, this formulation is only a part of a true description of Dickens' artistic solution. If he strategically sets aside the possibility of "totalization," he nonetheless embraces an overview of another kind:

Paul had never risen from his little bed. He lay there, listening to the noises in the street, quite tranquilly; not caring much how the time went, but watching it and watching everything about him with observing eyes.

When the sunbeams struck into his room through the rustling blinds, and quivered on the opposite wall like golden water, he knew that evening was coming on, and that the sky was red and beautiful. As the reflection died away, and a gloom went creeping up the wall, he watched it deepen, deepen, deepen, into night. Then he thought how the long streets were dotted with lamps, and how the peaceful stars were shining overhead. His fancy had a strange tendency to wander to the river, which he knew was flowing through the great city; and now he thought how black it was, and how deep it would look, reflecting the hosts of stars—and more than all, how steadily it rolled away to meet the sea.

As it grew later in the night, and footsteps in the street became so rare that he could hear them coming, count them as they passed, and lose them in the hollow distance, he would lie and watch the many-coloured ring about the candle, and wait patiently for day . . .

When day began to dawn again, he watched for the sun; and when its cheerful light began to sparkle in the room, he pictured to himself—pictured! he saw—the high church towers rising up into the morning sky, the town reviving, waking, starting into life once more, the river glistening as it rolled (but rolling fast as ever), and the country bright with dew. Familiar sounds and cries came by degrees into the street below.   (xvi, 220–21)

It is not less true of the "good" characters than of the "bad" that their purview is limited. Paul's confinement to what will be his deathbed radically restricts what he is able literally to see. But the above, at the beginning of the chapter which tells "What the Waves were always saying," goes mainly to show how much, rather than how little, he can make out about the outlying world as it is reflected and refracted within the narrow and shrinking parameters of his experience. The light rising and falling on the wall opposite the window, footsteps, the wheels of carts, cries. These are the diminished signs of an outer, extensive reality, the fullness of which Paul can no longer know. Yet somehow they afford him an apprehension of that greater reality, which he grasps not only, to some extent, in its particularity—"the high church towers rising up into the morning sky, the town reviving"—but also in its boundlessness: the ceaseless rush of the river toward the sea. From what does the gift of such a vision arise?

Plainly it is not the Balzacian overview that Paul here enjoys. To show this, one need only compare Paul's vision of the city to Rastignac's literal survey of Paris from a hilltop in the conclusion of *Père Goriot,* although it is not without significance that Rastignac's, too, is a view from the graveyard. Rastignac's is ambitious knowledge, an intended "stitching together," again, of information by which the city may be understood, and so conquered. Paul's genius is, of course, resignation: acceptance of, even loyalty to, one's constitutive limitations. Especially he is loyal to himself in the character of one who knows he has been created only to die. As such, he brings new meaning to his father's dictum that everyone should understand his own position.

We are near here to the great significance of Paul's diminutive tragedy. It is his crucial role to convey that, if our "home" or room, our metaphorical "situation," ex-

presses our limitations, our smallness, it also constitutes
our special advantage, our privilege—even in the profound sense in which the late Abraham Heschel observed
that it is a privilege to die. To our limitedness, as to our
mortality, we owe the very idea of our identity and the
prerogative of having or being a self. What I have called
Paul's loyalty is really loyalty of the most difficult and exalted kind because, paradoxically, it is loyalty to a reality,
an unglamorous matter of fact—his death—not to an abstraction or ideal. And his loyalty to the real does not go
unrewarded. Reflected off the wall of his room, drifting
in through his window, and announcing itself to us in
the modest periods of the above prose, is a gift of something precious. It is given to Paul to imagine the world as
it really is.

3

Paul's transcendent wisdom, of which so much is
made in the novel, is in fact ignorance—the ignorance of
Socrates. [12] It is the wisdom, in other words, of not having answers, of abounding in questions: What is the "old
fashion," death? What are the waves saying? "Floy, are
we *all* dead, except you?" (xvi, 223). It is not surprising,
of course, that Paul's simplicity should be problematic for
his elders. That it is centrally and profoundly problematic
for his father—"Papa! what's money?" (viii, 93)—is only
too apparently at the heart of the novel to need comment
here. But not so obvious perhaps is the contrast provided
to the characterization of Dombey Senior by his son's almost heroic understanding and acceptance of his own
ephemerality. It is by virtue of this acceptance that Paul

is able to transcend, in his deathbed visions, the fragmentation that pervades the imagination of the novel. He
transcends it, that is, precisely because he is willing to
accept that he himself is a fragment with slight and imperfect connections to the tangible world. Against this
stands the world-consciousness of Dombey Senior, like
Balzac's in its will to wholeness, like Rastignac's in that
Romantic fervency with which it imagines itself at the
world's center:

And again he said "Dom-bey and Son," in exactly the same
tone as before.
  Those three words conveyed the one idea of Mr.
Dombey's life. The earth was made for Dombey and Son to
trade in, and the sun and moon were made to give them light.
Rivers and seas were formed to float their ships; rainbows
gave them promise of fair weather; winds blew for or against
their enterprises; stars and planets circled in their orbits, to
preserve inviolate a system of which they were the
centre. (i, 2)

It is relevant to the above figurative exposition of Mr.
Dombey's pride that we take note of the paradoxical
basis of his characterization generally. The paradox is
that although Dombey maintains a proud, hyperborean
exterior, he is nonetheless a character portrayed throughout almost entirely in terms of his emotions. This is so
not only because of the strength of the emotional life
with which he is endowed, but also and especially because of his embarrassment at the fact of his emotions. We
see him everywhere obsessed with their suppression and
concealment.[13] The display of emotion in others is often
enough to summon his embarrassment. Here he witnesses
the deathbed embrace of Florence and her mother:

The child had run towards her; and, standing on tiptoe, the better to hide her face in her embrace, had clung about her with a desperate affection very much at variance with her years.

"Oh Lord bless me!" said Mr. Dombey, rising testily. "A very ill-advised and feverish proceeding this, I am sure. Please to ring there for Miss Florence's nurse. Really the person should be more careful. Wait! I had better ask Doctor Peps if he'll have the goodness to step upstairs again perhaps. I'll go down. I'll go down." (i, 3; with emendations for MS according to note.)

This is by no means the only occasion on which Dombey loses his famous composure. The reserve which marks his demeanor in the public, official views of him—at family ceremonies, in society, at the offices of the firm— should not mislead us on this point. Nor is what appears in such lapses mere squeamish indignation. Rather, they testify to a sensitivity that is surprisingly subtle and self-knowing:

The last time he had seen his slighted child, there had been that in the sad embrace between her and her dying mother, which was at once a revelation and a reproach to him. Let him be as absorbed as he would in the Son on whom he built such high hopes, he could not forget that closing scene. He could not forget that he had had no part in it. That, at the bottom of its clear depths of tenderness and truth, lay those two figures clasped in each other's arms, while he stood on the bank above them, looking down a mere spectator—not a sharer with them—quite shut out. (iii, 31)

He shows himself here sensible of a desire to be included in the flow of feeling between Florence and her mother. And he senses, too, that his exclusion constitutes a "reproach," not to the woman or the girl, but to himself. Of course, he would turn away such knowledge:

Unable to exclude these things from his remembrance, or to keep his mind free from such imperfect shapes of the meaning with which they were fraught, as were able to make themselves visible to him through the mist of his pride, his previous feeling of indifference towards little Florence changed into an uneasiness of an extraordinary kind. Young as she was, and possessing in any eyes but his (and perhaps in his too) even more than the usual amount of childish simplicity and confidence he almost felt as if she watched and distrusted him. As if she held the clue to something secret in his breast, of the nature of which he was hardly informed himself. As if she had an innate knowledge of one jarring and discordant string within him, and her very breath could sound it.   (iii, 31; with emendations for MS A)

The metaphors of vision have here the importance they so often have in Dickens: "such imperfect shapes of the meaning . . . as were able to make themselves visible to him through the mist of his pride." Especially they support the contrast between Dombey and his son, the novel's most gifted seer, a contrast which is reflected in their respective relations to Florence. Florence, too, is a seer. Dombey's "one jarring and discordant string," of which Florence is said to have "innate" and secret knowledge, is presumably his great suppressed susceptibility and needfulness, which her awareness of her own need for his love has enabled her to see. Her constant seeking of his favor is one of the things which links her to the visionary Paul, who spends his final weeks in Brighton quite openly seeking the love and affection of the "young gentlemen" and their keepers (xiv). This complex triangle, it appears, establishes once again that in Dickens' novels the ability to see "things as they really are" is associated with an avowal of insufficiency and contingency in the seer—in this case, of the need for love. Thus Paul's piercing vision, his sister's insight, and his father's blindness.

In pondering Dombey's blindness, we find ourselves in the presence of yet another negative paradigm of representation. Any pretension to wholeness or sufficiency, such as Dombey's, will undermine the subject's capacity to conceive or to grasp the real nature of any person or thing—and so it is with texts too satisfied with their own perceptual or representational capacities. Earlier in this study, we encountered in Bradley Headstone another character whose pretended self-sufficiency, and whose rigidly exclusive and repressive consciousness had implications for the novel's awareness of its own limits, its own exclusion and repression of reality by form. Headstone and Dombey have something else in common that is relevant to this body of implications: the preponderance of will in their constitution. Haughty self-reliance and taut, unyielding determination: such "hypertrophy of the will" [14] Dickens is exceptionally able to dramatize, and he inclines to do so, suggestively, as a category of passion. But its antithesis is also dramatized, in Lizzie Hexam as in Paul and Florence. To match the above passion, these latter have a solemn intensity of their own, a determination no less inexhaustible. But their determination proceeds in just the opposite direction—that is, towards a demonstration of limitation, of relatedness and dependence.

It is in terms of time that both novels test these profoundly different orientations of the will. Headstone, we recall, was at pains to deny the fact of his past, whereas it is the inevitability of the future that Dombey resists, when it is clear that the future will be different from what he has wished. Lizzie Hexam, by contrast, submits with reverence to the continuum of past, present, and future. Both actively and in her visions she seeks to affirm what I have called her openness to the fact of temporality, as in her feeling that responsibilities incurred by her dead father are now hers—a relationship to the dead that cannot help but remind us of Florence. And Paul is nowhere more moving, perhaps, than in his firm, quiet refusal to be falsely encouraged to see his future as other than what it is: an early death.

Dickens' novels give evidence on every level of his awareness of the supreme arrogation of the will upon which the act of writing the novel of reality is founded. The awareness is reflected in, is a dimension of, the internal workings out of the problem of will in the novels: in conflicts of opposing wills, in the welter of obstinacies, in the vauntings of mastery and submission. Doubtless the energy and thoroughness of presentation of Dombey and Headstone suggest Dickens' own identification, to some extent, with those overbearing and imperious models of the human will; but there is no mistaking which way his art, in the last analysis, truly inclines.

This chapter begins with a description of *Dombey and Son* as Dickens' "domestic" novel, the novel in which he gives his fullest and most earnest attention to an epitomized version of the contemporary life of his own class. The course of argument has not been to show in what exactitude of resemblance to literal reality his attention to everyday life ultimately issued. Of course the novel is not devoid of "realism" in this sense. The account of changes

in British life caused by the building of the railroad is
one instance of it, and the persuasiveness of Dombey's
characterization—"as actual as flesh and blood," as a
contemporary reviewer put it, to Dickens' immense delight[15]—is another. But my concern has been to inves-
tigate another kind of relationship to reality in the novel,
equal in importance to verisimilitude, and equal at least
in its claims to the denomination of "realism." It has
been my purpose to show that the novel takes as one of
its central, explicit concerns the access to reality, the ability to perceive the truth, of those who live life under the
conditions it illustrates and describes; to show, moreover, how the novel's chief characterizations as well as its
landscape and action are informed by the theme of realism; how the latter influences and finally even deter-
mines, perhaps, the form of the novel's own representation of the world.

When the impact of Dickens' treatment of this theme
has been gathered, it is unmistakable how different it is
from Flaubert's exaltation of the bourgeois life, "*Ils sont
dans le vrai!*" Dombeyism, no less than *le Bovarisme*, is an
epitomization of life behind the closed doors and shut-
tered windows of the bourgeois home, an allegory of the
sufficiency-unto-itself of the Victorian hearth; and it is
the emotional and spiritual experience of *le vrai*, precisely, that Dombeyism mitigates against. Paul manages
only to die, and not to live, with his visions. Otherwise
characters stand, like the Major, in the shade of their own
limitations, peering out at the incomprehensible, the
changing, the obscure. Of course, unlike the Major, some
characters are capable of taking their limitations into account. Toots is, as he says himself, confused, but he is

sane and steady enough not to imagine himself otherwise. Dombey, at the other extreme, lives the most wilfully self-deceiving of fictions. He requires an avalanche of melodrama to be budged from the conviction that his "position" in the world is central and commanding—that he is, in Bagstock's words, a "man of the world," who has lived in the world and knows the world.

Flaubert's interesting remark, as Mann makes us feel, has about it the nostalgic, idealizing overtones of exile, and in the present context it will perhaps remind us of one of the novel's subtlest rejoinders to Dombey's pride: the description of his painful awareness of his own exile from the community of feeling between Florence and her mother. The irony of the idea of Dombey as outsider is resonant with Dickens' deepest insights into the life of his epoch. Dickens himself belongs to, and he is writing to and about, that class at the acme of which Dombey stands in his success. But what Dickens chooses to depict in Dombey is the lonely isolation and emotional poverty of the "mercantile ideal." [16] From the beginning, however, he is surrounded in his loneliness by small, seemingly underground enclaves of community and sympathy—the Midshipman's table, the Toodle home, Florence and Susan Nipper, the house of Carker the Junior and his sister. Each of these suffers, in a different way, the pains of exile and separation, and each survives. Ultimately, of course—and perhaps too obviously—Dombey's own survival turns upon his conversion from an arrogant ideal of self-sufficiency to an ideal of dependence and community.

Dickens does offer, then, to Dombey and to the reader as well, the prospect of a community of feeling and of a viable relation to the real. Indeed, it is in such a community that the novel locates its own readily apparent sympathies, and in such a relation to the real that the novel hopes itself to stand. The way to describe what these are is to describe what they have in common, and what they have in common is structural, in the deepest sense. It may be stated as follows. The individual stands in relation to others as the work of art stands in relation to the world. Its limits are its identity. It is shaped by "the other"—by what it excludes, by what it is not. What the individual owes to others, what the work of imagination owes to the real world, is nothing less than its life. Thus little Paul addresses his question to the one whose acknowledgement of the fact of her dependence and relationship is most active and profound: "Floy, are we *all* dead, except you?"

Florence's self-denial and the spirit of Dickens' art are not the same, but in their similarity is the source of all that is alive and compelling in the novels. Unlike Florence, the art of Dickens is mightily unembarrassed, pleased with itself and celebratory of its own powers. It is also, however, decisively aware of its limitations, and its ultimate fidelity is not to itself.

Notes

Introduction: The Horizon of Etcetera

1. Forster, *The Life of Charles Dickens*, I, 394.

2. Lukács, *The Historical Novel*, pp. 243–44; Wellek, *Concepts of Criticism*, p. 255.

3. Ford, in *Dickens and His Readers*, discusses Turgenieff's admiration for Dickens, pp. 191–92, and the relation between Dickens' work and Henry James more extensively, pp. 203–12. Of numerous studies of Dickens' influence on Tolstoy, the shrewdest is probably that of F. R. and Q. D. Leavis in *Dickens the Novelist*, pp. 34–106. Tolstoy once wrote that Dickens was "the greatest writer of the nineteenth century," in a letter to N. Gusev, Feb. 3, 1904. See Gusev, "Dickens and Tolstoy," trans. E. Bernstein, *The Dickensian*, No. 28 (Winter 1932), p. 64.

4. On Dickens and Dostoyevsky's "higher realism," see Fanger, *Dostoyevsky and Romantic Realism*, especially ch. 3. The most important study of Dickens' novels as constituting a world in themselves is Miller, *Charles Dickens: The World of His Novels*.

5. Watt, *The Rise of the Novel*, especially pp. 9–34.

6. Watt, *The Rise of the Novel*, p. 11.

7. The phrase is from Wellek, *Concepts of Criticism*, p. 255. For Trilling see his essay on *Little Dorrit* (1953), repr. in *Dickens: A Collection of Critical Essays*, ed. Martin Price (Englewood Cliffs, N.J.: Prentice-Hall, 1967). See also my remarks on the formalist bias of Trilling's essay in

chapter 3. For Van Ghent, see her reading of *Great Expectations* (1950) in *The English Novel*.

8. Cf. Watt, *The Rise of the Novel,* pp. 11–12.

1. Form in the Realist Novel: *War and Peace* and *Our Mutual Friend*

1. The translation used here is that of Louise and Aylmer Maude in the Inner Sanctum Ed. (New York: Simon and Schuster, 1942). References are to book, chapter, page of that edition: (i, i, 1).

2. See Georg Lukács, "Tolstoy and the Development of Realism," *Studies in European Realism,* p. 182.

3. Wellek and Warren, *Theory of Literature,* p. 241.

4. *Ibid.,* p. 25.

5. See *ibid.,* p. 246.

6. Wellek, *Concepts of Criticism,* p. 255.

7. Brady, "Fact and Factuality in Literature," p. 109, n. 3.

8. Napoleon's decision to go to war with Russia, for example, can be compared, in the arbitrariness that Tolstoy attributes to it, to the mock-serious decision of Andrew to marry Natásha when he sees her at a ball: "If she goes to her cousin first, and then to another lady, she will be my wife" (vi, ix, 506).

9. See *The Letters of Henry James,* 2 vols., ed. Percy Lubbock (New York: Scribner's, 1920), ii, 237, 324.

10. See Christian, *Tolstoy: A Critical Introduction,* pp. 102–03.

11. Cited in Christian, *Tolstoy's War and Peace,* p. 21.

12. See Lukács, "Tolstoy and the Development of Realism," *Studies in European Realism,* p. 182.

13. Compare my idea of "open form" with its different connotations in Adams, *Strains of Discord,* and Friedman, *The Turn of the Novel,* especially pp. 15–37.

14. Wellek, *Concepts of Criticism,* p. 255.

15. Frye, *Anatomy of Criticism,* p. 134.

16. Cited in Ford, *Dickens and His Readers,* p. 134.

17. Cited *ibid.,* p. 136. Ford, however, takes this to be addressed to the matter of linguistic exaggeration: to "readers who refuse to admit the desirability of stylization in fiction." This is a reading to which Ford's notion of Dickens as "poet" obliges him. Ch. 7 of Ford's book, called "The Poet and the Critics of Probability," is invaluable for discussions of Dickens' realism.

18. Frye is a more subtle reader of Dickens than his random remarks in the *Anatomy* suggest. See his "Dickens and the Comedy of Humours" in *The Stubborn Structure,* pp. 218–40.

19. Frye, *Anatomy of Criticism,* p. 140.

20. Chesterton, *Appreciations and Criticisms of Charles Dickens' Works,* p. 212. Counting by changes of set, the dining room scene is actually the third.

21. Cf. J. Hillis Miller, "Afterward" to *Our Mutual Friend* (New York: New American Library, 1964), pp. 905–6. Also Miller, *The Form of Victorian Fiction,* pp. 37–41.

22. James, "The Limitations of Dickens," pp. 49–50.

23. *Ibid.,* p. 51.

24. Arnold Kettle, *"Our Mutual Friend,"* in *Dickens and the Twentieth Century,* ed. John Gross and Gabriel Pearson (Toronto: University of Toronto Press, 1962), p. 220.

25. James, "The Limitations of Dickens," pp. 50–51.

26. See Trilling, *Beyond Culture,* p. 196.

27. James, "The Limitations of Dickens," p. 52.

28. The Mortimer narration is a good example of what David Thorburn has recently called "the drama of the telling," in his essay, "Fiction and Imagination in *Don Quixote.*" "This insistence on the limits of the book we hold in our hands, and especially the recurring tactic of allowing the novel's several narrators to intrude into Quixote's story and to interrupt it, deflects attention toward what might be called *the drama of the telling:* a drama concerned not with the protagonist's adventures themselves but with the problems and difficulties of writing about them." Thorburn goes on to suggest that there is a tradition of "self-reflexiveness" in the English novel, which includes "certain major works of Dickens" as well as Conrad, Joyce, and Woolf (p. 437).

29. Lukács, *The Theory of the Novel,* pp. 38–39.

30. Cf. Lukács, *The Historical Novel,* pp. 243–44.

31. The phrase is from Martin Price, "The Irrelevant Detail and the Emergence of Form," p. 75: "In *The Sense of an Ending,* Frank Kermode draws a sharp distinction between the simplicity of myths and the skeptical testing of that pattern against the contingencies of the actual. Only in such testing can myths be disconfirmed, and the result of such discomfirmation will be those reversals or pereties Aristotle finds in complex plots. The need to readjust expectations earns the mature fiction that incorporates contingencies without despairing of form. The myths of which Mr. Kermode writes—and there are some who would call them by a less cherished name—have often been adapted wishfully and conventionally to the more familiar situations of contemporary life, converting archetype into stereotype. It is these generalized forms with which the realistic novel always quarrels, breaking their limits by extension, and insisting upon the stubbornness of the actual."

32. Miller, *Charles Dickens: The World of His Novels,* p. 238.

2. The Hollow Down by the Flare: *Our Mutual Friend* Continued

1. Bertolt Brecht, "Against Georg Lukács," repr. in *New Left Review* 84 March–April 1974), 41.

2. See J. Hillis Miller, "Afterward" to *Our Mutual Friend* (New York: New American Library, 1964), pp. 909–10.

3. Grahame Smith, *Dickens, Money, and Society* (Berkeley and Los Angeles: University of California Press, 1968), p. 183.

4. Watt, *The Rise of the Novel,* p. 52.

5. James, "The Limitations of Dickens," p. 52.

6. See Martin Price's discussion of "impulse" vs. "culture" in the novel, in "The Fictional Contract," *Literary Theory and Structure: Essays in Honor of William K. Wimsatt,* ed. Frank Brady, John Palmer, and Martin Price (New Haven and London: Yale University Press, 1973), especially pp. 163–65.

7. See Marcus, *Dickens: From Pickwick to Dombey,* p. 80.

8. Roman Jakobson (with Morris Halle), *Fundamentals of Language,* 2d ed., rev. (The Hague: Mouton, 1971), pp. 91–92.

9. On novels as "models" of outward reality, see Price, "The Fictional Contract," pp. 168–71.

10. I do not refer to the irony that, as Forster notes, Venus' shop is drawn from life. See *Life,* II, 292.

11. Price, "The Irrelevant Detail and the Emergence of Form," p. 74.

12. George Eliot, *Adam Bede,* Everyman Ed. (London: J. M. Dent, 1960), p. 174.

3. Words and Freedom: Dombey, Clennam, Nell

1. Cf. Thorburn, "Fiction and Imagination in *Don Quixote,*" p. 136.

2. See Roland Barthes, "To Write: An Intransitive Verb?" in *The Structuralists: From Marx to Lévi-Strauss,* ed. Richard T. De George and Fernande M. De George (Garden City, N.Y.: Anchor Books, 1972), pp. 155–67.

3. See J. Hillis Miller on the metonymic quality of Dickens' imagination in *Sketches by Boz,* in "The Fiction of Realism," especially pp. 93–98.

4. According to Peter Fairclough in his "Notes" in the Penguin edition of *Dombey and Son* (Hamondsworth: Penguin, 1970), p. 982.

5. Wilson, "Dickens: The Two Scrooges," pp. 1–104; Johnson, *Charles Dickens: His Tragedy and Triumph;* Graham Greene, "The Young Dickens" in *The Dickens Critics,* ed. George H. Ford and Lauriat Lane, Jr. (Ithaca, N.Y.: Cornell University Press, 1961), pp. 244–52.

6. Wilson, "Dickens: The Two Scrooges," p. 14.

7. Marcus, "Language into Structure," p. 189.

8. Marcus, "Language into Structure," p. 195.

9. Miller, "The Fiction of Realism," pp. 85–86.

10. Miller, "The Fiction of Realism," pp. 122–123, 92.

11. "Any literary text is both self-referential and extra-referential, or rather it is open to being not seen as the former and mistakenly taken as the latter." (Miller, p. 124).

12. See House, *The Dickens World*, pp. 123–25.

13. Wimsatt and Brooks, *Literary Criticism*, p. 755. According to the preface, the chapter in which this remark appears is by Wimsatt (p. xi).

14. Cleanth Brooks, *The Well-Wrought Urn* (New York: Harcourt, Brace, 1947), p. 75.

15. Lionel Trilling, "Little Dorrit," repr. in *Dickens: A Collection of Critical Essays*, ed. Martin Price (Englewood Cliffs, N.J.: Prentice-Hall, 1967), p. 147.

16. Davis, "The Sense of the Real in English Fiction," pp. 200–17.

17. Trilling, *The Opposing Self*, p. 94.

4. The Sentimental Criticism of Philosophy in *Oliver Twist*

1. Marcus, "Language into Structure," pp. 196–97.

2. Marcus, "Language into Structure," p. 201.

3. Graham Greene, "The Young Dickens," in *The Dickens Critics*, ed. George H. Ford and Lauriat Lane, Jr. (Ithaca, N.Y.: Cornell University Press, 1961), p. 248; Marcus, *Dickens: From Pickwick to Dombey*, pp. 29–30; Miller, *Charles Dickens: The World of His Novels*, p. 43.

4. Sylvère Monod, *Dickens the Novelist* (Norman: University of Oklahoma Press, 1968), pp. 120–21.

5. House, *The Dickens World*, Chs. iii and iv, but especially pp. 69–70; Williams, *Culture and Society*, pp. 92–97.

6. In the *Autobiography*, cited by House, p. 69.

7. A notable exception is Alexander Welsh, *The City of Dickens* (Oxford: Clarendon, 1971), which contains chapters on the "hearth" and what Welsh calls "The Spirit of Love and Truth." The approach is sociological.

8. Williams, "Dickens and Social Ideas," pp. 89–91.

9. Miller, *Charles Dickens: The World of His Novels*, p. 36; Marcus, *Dickens: From Pickwick to Dombey*, p. 64.

10. See J. Hillis Miller, "Introduction" to *Oliver Twist* (New York: Holt, Rinehart, and Winston, 1962).

11. Of course Boz, even Boz at Newgate in the *Sketches,* was never only a muckraker. But just as the *Sketches* show that Dickens' sheerly verbal virtuosity is at his command from the outset of his career, so also they manifest that diligent attempt to manipulate our emotional responses which never departs for long from Dickens' later work.

12. Williams speaks of Dickens' "Whole drama of values, the powerful way of seeing the world so that it cannot but be criticized and responded to," in "Social Criticism in Dickens," pp. 214–17.

5. The Novel of Reality: *Dombey and Son*

1. Forster, *The Life of Charles Dickens,* I, 296.

2. Johnson, *Charles Dickens: His Tragedy and Triumph,* I, 470.

3. Cited in Williams, "Social Criticism in Dickens," p. 221.

4. Thomas Mann, "Homage," trans. Eithne Wilkins and Ernst Kaiser, in the "Definitive Edition" of *The Castle* by Franz Kafka, trans. Willa and Edwin Muir, Modern Library Ed. (New York: Random House, 1969), pp. xi-xvii.

5. Mann, "Homage," p. x.

6. Mann, "Homage," p. xi.

7. Compare, however, G. K. Chesterton's opinion: "The incurable poetic character, the hopelessly non-realistic character of Dickens' essential genius could not have a better example than the story of the Dombeys. For the story itself is probable; it is the treatment that makes it unreal. In attempting to paint the dark pagan devotion of the father (as distinct from the ecstatic and Christian devotion of the mother) Dickens was painting something that was really there. This is no wild theme, like the wanderings of Nell's grandfather, or the marriage of Gride. A man of Dombey's type would love his son as he loves Paul. He would neglect his daughter as he neglects Florence. And yet we feel the utter unreality of it all, while we feel the utter reality of monsters like Stiggins or Mantalini. Dickens could only work in his own way, and that way was the wild way. We may almost say this: that he could only make his characters probable if he was allowed to make them impossible. Give him licence to say and do anything, and he could create beings as vivid as our own aunts and uncles. Keep him to likelihood and he could not tell the plainest tale so as to make it seem likely. The

story of "Pickwick" is credible, although it is not possible. The story of Florence Dombey is incredible although it is true." In *Charles Dickens*, pp. 297–98.

8. See Marcus, *Dickens: From Pickwick to Dombey*, pp. 297–98.

9. See, for example, the descriptions of Twemlow in *Our Mutual Friend*, Tom Pinch in *Martin Chuzzlewit*, and Pickwick. All three are "old-fashioned" in their attire, and their benevolent spirit is identified with the Georgian period.

10. "Thou hast no speculation in those eyes/ Which thou does glare with!" *Macbeth* III.iv. Peter Fairclough, in his notes to the Penguin edition of the novel, finds four direct allusions to *Macbeth*. There are also references to *Henry IV* and to *Hamlet*—both, incidentally or not, Sons and Heirs like Paul. In general, perhaps more in evidence here than in any other Dickens novel except *The Old Curiosity Shop* is the novelist's familiarity with Shakespeare.

11. See especially Marcus' chapter on *Dombey*, "The Changing World," in *Dickens: From Pickwick to Dombey*, pp. 293–357.

12. Compare the connotations, here, of the term "transcendence" with those which emerge from a contrast of Dickens and Eliot by Raymond Williams. In Eliot he finds "the virtues of a positivist analytic and referential mode—the very strengths of intellectual liberalism," whereas in Dickens he finds "an alternative radicalism, . . . a central human vision of goodness and kindness and fullness of life which then creatively transcends, is made to transcend and surpass, the expositions and rationalizations of temporary interests—a movement, one may say, of conversion rather than persuasion, and of acts of transcendence rather than of conclusion" ("Dickens and Social Ideas," p. 87).

13. In the Preface of 1867, Dickens observed that the "two commonest mistakes in judgment" were "the confounding of shyness with arrogance . . . and the not understanding that an obstinate nature exists in a perpetual struggle with itself." (p. 834)

14. Marcus, *Dickens: From Pickwick to Dombey*, p. 321.

15. The review by Charles Kent appeared in *The Sun*, April 13, 1848. Ford, *Dickens and His Readers*, p. 265.

16. Wilson, "Dickens: The Two Scrooges," p. 31.

Selected Bibliography

The following is a list of secondary sources I have found especially useful or suggestive in my study of Dickens, realism, and the novel form.

Adams, Robert M. *Strains of Discord: Studies in Literary Openness.* Ithaca, N.Y.: Cornell University Press, 1958.

Alter, Robert. *Fielding and the Nature of the Novel.* Cambridge, Mass.: Harvard University Press, 1968.

Auerbach, Erich. *Mimesis: The Representation of Reality in Western Literature.* Trans. Willard R. Trask. Princeton, N.J.: Princeton University Press, 1953.

Bayley, John. *"Oliver Twist:* 'Things as They Really Are.' " In *Dickens and the Twentieth Century,* ed. John Gross and Gabriel Pearson. Toronto: University of Toronto Press, 1962.

—— *Tolstoy and the Novel.* New York: Viking, 1967.

Becker, George, ed. *Documents of Modern Literary Realism.* Princeton, N.J.: Princeton University Press, 1967.

Benjamin, Walter. "The Storyteller." In *Illuminations,* ed. with introduction by Hannah Arendt. Trans. Harry Zohn. New York: Schocken, 1969.

Booth, Wayne C. *The Rhetoric of Fiction.* Chicago and London: University of Chicago Press, 1961.

Brady, Frank. "Fact and Factuality in Literature." In *Directions in Literary Criticism,* ed. Stanley Weintraub and Philip Young. University Park and London: Pennsylvania State University Press, 1973.

Chesterton, G. K. *Appreciations and Criticisms of Charles Dickens' Works*. New York: Dutton, 1911.

—— *Charles Dickens*. Introduction by Steven Marcus. New York: Schocken, 1965.

Christian, R. F. *Tolstoy's War and Peace*. Oxford: Clarendon Press, 1962.

—— *Tolstoy: A Critical Introduction*. Cambridge, Eng.: The University Press, 1969.

Davis, Robert Gorham. "The Sense of the Real in English Fiction." *Comparative Literature* 3 (Summer 1951): 200–17.

Ellmann, Richard, and Charles Feidelson, Jr., eds. *The Modern Tradition: Backgrounds of Modern Literature*. New York: Oxford University Press, 1965. Especially pp. 228–378.

Engel, Monroe. *The Maturity of Dickens*. Cambridge, Mass.: Harvard University Press, 1959.

Fanger, Donald. *Dostoyevsky and Romantic Realism: A Study of Dostoyevsky in Relation to Balzac, Dickens, and Gogol*. Chicago: University of Chicago Press, 1967.

Flibbert, Joseph T. "Dickens and the French Debate over Realism." *Comparative Literature* 23 (1971): 18–31.

Ford, George H. *Dickens and His Readers: Aspects of Novel Criticism Since 1836*. Princeton, N.J.: Princeton University Press, 1955.

Forster, John. *The Life of Charles Dickens*. 2 vols. Everyman ed. London: J. M. Dent, 1927.

Friedman, Alan. *The Turn of the Novel*. New York: Oxford University Press, 1966.

Frye, Northrop. *Anatomy of Criticism: Four Essays*. Princeton, N.J.: Princeton University Press, 1957.

—— *The Stubborn Structure*. London: Methuen, 1970.

Gissing, George. *Charles Dickens*. New York: Dodd, Mead, 1924.

Hardy, Barbara. *The Appropriate Form: An Essay on the Novel*. London: University of London, Atholone Press, 1964.

Harvey, W. J. *Character and the Novel*. Ithaca, N.Y.: Cornell University Press, 1965.

Holloway, John. "Dickens and the Symbol." In *Dickens 1970*, ed. Michael Slater. New York: Stein and Day, 1970.

House, Humphrey. *The Dickens World*. 2d ed. Oxford, London, New York: Oxford University Press, 1960.

James, Henry. "The Limitations of Dickens," Review of *Our*

Mutual Friend. In *The Dickens Critics,* ed. George H. Ford and Lauriat Lane, Jr. Ithaca, N.Y.: Cornell University Press, 1961.

Johnson, Edgar. *Charles Dickens: His Tragedy and Triumph.* 2 vols. New York: Simon and Schuster, 1952.

Kermode, Frank. *The Sense of an Ending: Studies in the Theory of Fiction.* New York: Oxford University Press, 1967.

Killham, John. "Autonomy Versus Mimesis?" *The British Journal of Aesthetics* 7, No. 3 (July 1967): 274–85.

Leavis, F. R. and Q. D. *Dickens the Novelist.* New York: Pantheon, 1970.

Lukács, Georg. *Studies in European Realism.* Trans. Edith Bone. London: Hillway, 1950.

—— *The Historical Novel.* Trans. Hannah and Stanley Mitchell. London: Merlier Press, 1962.

—— *The Theory of the Novel.* Trans. Anna Bostock. London: Merlier Press, 1971.

—— *Realism in Our Time: Literature and the Class Struggle.* Trans. John and Necke Mander. Preface by George Steiner. New York, Evanston, San Francisco, London: Harper and Row, 1971.

—— *Writer and Critic and Other Essays.* Ed. and trans. Arthur D. Kahn. New York: Grosset and Dunlap, 1971.

Marcus, Steven. *Dickens: From Pickwick to Dombey.* New York: Simon and Schuster, Clarion Books, 1968.

—— "Language into Structure: Pickwick Revisited." *Dedalus,* 101, No. 1 (Winter 1972): 183–202.

Miller, J. Hillis. *Charles Dickens: The World of His Novels.* Cambridge, Mass.: Harvard University Press, 1965.

—— *The Form of Victorian Fiction: Thackeray, Dickens, Trollope, George Eliot, Meredith, and Hardy.* University of Notre Dame Ward-Phillips Lecture in English Language and Literature, ii. Notre Dame, Ind. and London: University of Notre Dame Press, 1968.

—— "The Fiction of Realism: *Sketches by Boz, Oliver Twist,* and Cruikshank's Illustrations." In *Dickens Centennial Essays,* ed. Ada Nisbet and Blake Nevius. Berkeley, Los Angeles, and London: University of California Press, 1971.

Ortega y Gasset, José. *The Dehumanization of Art and Notes on the Novel.* Trans. Helene Weyl. Princeton, N.J.: Princeton University Press, 1948.

Poggioli, Renato. "Tolstoy as Man and Artist." *The Spirit of the Letter: Essays in European Literature.* Cambridge, Mass.: Harvard University Press, 1965.

Price, Martin. "The Irrelevant Detail and the Emergence of Form." In *Aspects of Narrative: Selected Papers from the English Institute,* ed. J. Hillis Miller. New York: Columbia University Press, 1971.

—— "The Fictional Contract." In *Literary Theory and Structure: Essays in Honor of William K. Wimsatt,* ed. Frank Brady, John Palmer, and Martin Price. New Haven, Conn. and London: Yale University Press, 1973.

Scholes, Robert and Robert Kellogg. *The Nature of Narrative.* London, Oxford, and New York: Oxford University Press, 1971.

Spilka, Mark. *Dickens and Kafka: A Mutual Interpretation.* London: Denis Dobson, 1963.

Steiner, George. *Tolstoy or Dostoyevsky: An Essay in the Old Criticism.* New York: Dutton, 1971.

Stern, J. P. *On Realism.* London and Boston: Routledge and Kegan Paul, 1973.

Taine, Hippolyte. *History of English Literature.* Trans. H. Van Laun. New York: Ungar, 1965. IV, 115–64.

Thorburn, David. "Fiction and Imagination in *Don Quixote*." *Partisan Review* (1975), no. 3, pp. 431–43.

Trilling, Lionel. *The Opposing Self: Nine Essays in Critism.* New York: Viking, 1955.

—— *Beyond Culture.* New York: Viking, 1968.

Van Ghent, Dorothy. *The English Novel: Form and Function.* New York: Harper and Row, Perennial Library, 1967.

—— "The Dickens World: A View from Todgers." In *Dickens: A Collection of Critical Essays,* ed. Martin Price. Englewood Cliffs, N.J.: Prentice-Hall, 1967.

Watt, Ian. *The Rise of the Novel.* Berkeley, Los Angeles, and London: University of California Press, 1957.

Wellek, René and Austin Warren. *Theory of Literature.* 3d ed. New York: Harcourt, Brace, and World, 1956.

Wellek, René. *Concepts of Criticism.* Ed. Stephen G. Nichols, Jr. New Haven and London: Yale University Press, 1963.

Williams, Raymond. *Culture and Society: 1780–1954.* New York: Harper and Row, 1958.

—— "Social Criticism in Dickens: Some Problems of Method

and Approach." *Critical Quarterly* 6 (Autumn 1964): 214–27.

——— "Dickens and Social Ideas." In *Dickens 1970,* ed. Michael Slater. New York: Stein and Day, 1970.

Wilson, Edmund. "Dickens: The Two Scrooges." *The Wound and the Bow.* Corrected ed. New York: Oxford University Press, 1947.

Wimsatt, William K., Jr. and Cleanth Brooks. *Literary Criticism: A Short History.* New York: Knopf, 1959.

Index

Abbreviations for titles of Dickens' novels are as follows:

Pickwick Papers: PP
Oliver Twist: OT
Nicholas Nickleby: NN
The Old Curiosity Shop: OCS
Martin Chuzzlewit: MC
Dombey and Son: DS
David Copperfield: DC
Bleak House: BH
Little Dorrit: LD
Great Expectations: GE
Our Mutual Friend: OMF

DATE DUE